"Americans and freedom-loving people everywhere currently find themselves in the midst of an unprecedented war on the very foundations and fabric of that which freedom resides. Yet attempts to confront this enemy according to conventional means are as futile as going up against battleships with bayonets. With military expertise and precision, General Michael Flynn and Sergeant Boone Cutler have crafted *The Citizen's Guide to Fifth Generation Warfare* to properly equip humanity to understand and effectively engage the enemy we face. This is a tool that should be in the home of every patriotic family across the globe. It is an invaluable resource for those who seek to carry on this battle and uphold our heartfelt intent to preserve, protect and defend the sovereignty of our nations against the globalist new world order."

CHRISTOPHER G. ADAMO | AUTHOR
Rules for Defeating Radicals: Countering the Alinsky Strategy in Politics and Culture

THE CITIZEN'S GUIDE TO
FIFTH GENERATION WARFARE

Introduction to 5GW
Session 1

Michael T. Flynn, LTG, U.S. Army, (Retired)
Boone Cutler, SGT, U.S. Army, (Retired)

Every age has its own kind
of war, its own limiting conditions,
and its own peculiar preconceptions.

General Carl von Clausewitz
Military Theorist and Author of On War

Resilient Patriot, LLC
ISBN | 979-8-88862-758-7
Printed in the United States of America

THE CITIZEN'S GUIDE TO FIFTH GENERATION WARFARE

5 GW: Session 1
Contents

Preface

CHAPTER 3 Make Ready   Section

Preface

Free your mind...and your ass will follow.
Funkadelic

The Citizen's Guide to Fifth Generation Warfare is designed to educate the public on a form of warfare currently being waged against all of us: Americans and other freedom-loving nations around the world. In warfare, there are opposing sides and in Fifth Generation Warfare, identifying the adversaries is even more difficult due to the nature of the war itself.

Fifth Generation Warfare (5GW) is best defined as a war of narratives. This *Citizen's Guide* teaches how to break through the many narratives imposed on society today by an overreaching federal government, an out-of-control security state, a weaponized media, and corporate and social media titans.

The Citizen's Guide doesn't direct action. It simply exists to help readers understand the very complex nature of warfare in the simplest terms possible. It is designed for the layperson. As you read through the pages, you'll gain a deeper understanding of the dynamic battlespace upon which we are operating. Yes, we are at war, and the war is very real.

After reading this *Guide,* you should have a far deeper understanding of the principles and terms that surround and define 5GW, ideas about who the adversaries are and how they are arrayed to oppose our way of life. Lastly, we hope to present ideas about how to defeat this determined foe.

First, your neighbors are most likely not your enemy, regardless of their beliefs. They are just as confused by the same anxieties that you have. Any sort of violence against each other provides shadowy governments with the excuses and conditions to impose more restrictive rules and laws, as well as an ability to add increased numbers of people to enforce these laws. If you are reading this *Citizen's Guide,* the first thing to do is share this information, no matter what country you are in.

Your primary enemy is the shadowy government that is manipulating you to hate someone else. Arm your friends, neighbors, and even those whom you don't get along with. Provide them with this information and shake hands. Recruit even those you've seen as enemies to teach them what's happening so that for the first time in history, the mass of people worldwide can take back liberty for themselves in whatever country they live. It all starts with the proper education to make the appropriate plan and then execute that plan. And in today's global environment, it will take a worldwide citizenry to organize and mobilize smartly, civically, and professionally.

Governments cause wars; militaries and citizens do not. The phrase "It takes a network to defeat a network" has been applied to many topics and issues. In this instance, we are each other's allies. Our growing network of citizens worldwide must stand together against the network of globalist power brokers who wish to destroy the individual identities of nation-states to establish a new normal (aka the New World Order). If by chance real physical war begins with or between other nations, pray that we are ready. But let war come from consent of the governed, not from a mandate of those who were never legitimately elected.

Our fight today is not between people of different nations. Instead, it is the fight of all people against globalist oppressors who are trying to strip us of our individual national identities and the most basic of human rights. If we lose, it will be the end of freedom as we know it worldwide, and we will all live or die at the command of one rich king with an invisible hand. The plan of the oppressors is to create a defenseless people in borderless countries who have limited or nonexistent parental rights. Throughout this *Guide*, you will see how they plan to get there. One purpose of this *Guide* is to help you make smarter decisions based on a deeper understanding of what you're up against, instead of making decisions based on your emotions.

> *I'm for truth, no matter who tells it.*
> *I'm for justice, no matter who it is for or against.*
> *I'm a human being, first and foremost, and as such*
> *I'm for whoever and whatever benefits humanity as a whole.*
> Malcolm X | Assassinated Civil Rights Activist

Most people in all categories and walks of life are unaware of the information you'll find in this *Citizen's Guide.* With very few exceptions, this form of warfare is taught to a small segment of our military and to those working inside our national security organizations, such as the various components of the U.S. Intelligence Community. What we need to do as citizens is to read and understand this information and then challenge those who shape the environment around us.

We should assume that several categories of people know what is in this *Guide:* some of the specialized elements within our military, such as our special operations forces; some of those serving in the U.S. Intelligence community, such as inside the various security services —the Federal Bureau of Investigation, Central Intelligence Agency, National Security Agency, and Diplomatic Security Service. However, others who influence our daily lives won't have a clue typically of what you're talking about when it comes to 5GW. These include most lawmakers, many law enforcement officers, most religious leaders, most social media influencers you follow, most podcasters you listen to, and many military veterans.

Our responsibility as citizens is to challenge and inform those "leaders" in our communities and others we follow for our everyday news and information to gain a better understanding of what we're facing from an overreaching government. In that manner, we can inform them as to why they feel like something isn't quite right and why that feeling is difficult to identify. Lastly, this *Guide* is not only for the people of the United States of America, but it is also written as a guide for all freedom-loving people everywhere on planet earth.

It takes a network to defeat a network.

General Stanley McChrystal | U.S. Army (Retired)
Author of *Team of Teams: New Rules of Engagement for a Complex World*

Chapter 1
Important Terms to Know and Remember

1-1   FIFTH GENERATION WARFARE (5GW)

The modern era of warfare is called Fifth Generation Warfare (5GW) for a reason. When we discuss 5GW, it is a term of reference for the historic times we now face. Just like we have generational designations for people like Boomers, Gen X, Millennials, Gen Z, and so forth, we have similar designations for eras of warfare. We now face a time when the advancement of war has landed us squarely in Fifth Generation Warfare.

Inside the strategy and tactics of 5GW is manipulation of thoughts and attitudes without people's awareness. These are the weapons of choice to facilitate geopolitical goals to create a new world order. There are a lot of overlapping aspects of hybrid, irregular, and unrestricted warfare, and we listed each in hopes that you, the reader, will study them more closely on your own and return to this *Guide* routinely to understand more fully some of the issues which we are facing daily. And as you hear others describe some of the terms or as you sense some shift in the numerous narratives that bombard us daily, you'll know it's all in the ballpark of 5GW.

1-2   HYBRID WARFARE

Hybrid Warfare is political warfare that blends conventional warfare, irregular warfare, and cyberwarfare with other influencing methods, such as fake news, diplomacy, lawfare, and foreign electoral intervention. It is influencing a foreign government through the people of a country with contrived media, cyber disruption, corrupt legal processes, direct conventional military actions by state actors, irregular warfare by non-state actors, electoral interference, and diplomatic leverage.

1-3   IRREGULAR WARFARE

According to the Irregular Warfare Annex to the National Defense Strategy for the United States in 2020, "Irregular warfare is a struggle among state and non-state actors to influence populations and affect legitimacy . . . favors indirect and asymmetric approaches, though it may employ the full range of military and other capabilities to erode an adversary's power, influence, and will. It includes the specific missions of unconventional warfare." It does everything hybrid warfare does, but focuses primarily on the use of non-state actors conducting covert military actions rather than direct, conventional military actions.

1-4   UNRESTRICTED WARFARE

Unrestricted Warfare is war without bounds. It is the strategy tailored for covert influence across the global stage. Covert influence happens by concealing the methods of influence. It's the primary strategy originally developed by China's military. The elements of unrestricted warfare are network corruption, legal exploitation, and economic manipulation. Unrestricted warfare does everything irregular that hybrid warfare does, but it is specific to CCP's strategy to shape the entire global environment. Additionally, they incorporate massive influence with economic warfare.

The specific aspects listed herein from hybrid, irregular, and unrestricted warfare occur together in what are referred to as "grey-zone conflicts."

1-5   GENERATIONS OF WARFARE

There have been four previously defined generations of warfare dating back to the pre-Napoleonic era (circa 1700s), depending on who you ask. Arguments to the contrary, the important element to know is that with each advancement of technology or tactic also comes the advancement of warfare. For instance, the machine gun changed the nature of killing in WWI, just as the tank changed the nature of maneuver in WWII. And the nuclear bomb changed the nature of warfare forever. However, there is disagreement on the exact elements of each generation of warfare. For example:

1. **First generation warfare** is pre-gunpowder.

2. **Second generation warfare** introduced the aspect of weapons that used gunpowder.

3. **Third generation warfare** incorporated flying machines, tanks, trench warfare, rockets, and long-range artillery.

4. **Fourth generation warfare** introduced atomic and nuclear weapons, as well as the concept of state and non-state actors, including terrorists, seeking to achieve political goals on a global stage.

Chapter 1

5. **Fifth generation warfare** evolved when the overlap of hybrid, irregular, and unrestricted warfare became directed at societies to affect the cognitive battlespace: the belief system of civilians and other target audiences that equaled more value than just the geography or ideology of a nation or its leaders.

We recognize these latter aspects have existed in all generations of war throughout human history. However, in Fifth Generation Warfare they've now become the primary strategy and no longer play a supporting role.

1-6   THE GREY ZONE

Grey-zone conflicts occur in the contested arena somewhere between routine politically focused diplomatic activity and outright physical war. The concept of the grey zone is built on existing military strategies but stops short of all-out war. Artificial intelligence applications, current and emerging information technologies, and popular social media platforms and influencers have created radicalized new spaces which have expanded what was impossible only a decade ago. Modern hybrid, irregular, and unrestricted warfare operations primarily occur in the grey zone and are conducted by state and non-state actors. In select cases, they conduct these operations in coordination with each other.

1-7   PSYCHOLOGICAL OPERATIONS (PSYOP)

Psychological Operations (PSYOP) are operations designed to convey selective information and indicators to audiences to influence their emotions, motives, and objective reasoning in order to affect the behavior of governments, organizations, groups, and individuals.

1-8   TARGET AUDIENCE (TA)

According to the U.S. Department of Defense, a "Target Audience (TA) is an individual or group selected for influence or attack by means of psychological operations." TAs can be based on gender, position in a family (fathers, mothers, order of birth, etc.), tribal connections, political affiliations, religious background, economic standing, regional areas, age, military affiliation, occupation, educational background, and anything else that lumps people into a group.

After a PSYOP objective is determined and a PSYOP plan is made, various TAs will be assessed to determine how they can be influenced to support the PSYOP objectives. TA analysis seeks to answer key questions. Accurate and thorough analyses of the TA will yield the following vital information:

1.   What TAs will be most effective in accomplishing the supporting PSYOP objectives?

2.   What are the reasons for the TA's current behavior?
What are the best means of communication to reach the TA?

3.   How can the TA be influenced to achieve the desired behavior?

4.   What are the appropriate criteria by which to assess behavior change?

Right now, someone somewhere is assessing you as a "target" and figuring out how to influence your thoughts, behavior, and actions. There are military manuals written on how to do it. This is not new, and with the proliferation of artificial intelligence and social media, it's never been faster, easier, or more effective. Every click, every search, every hashtag, and every response you type on a machine hooked to the internet is a factor that develops a matrix for how best to manipulate you. Worldwide.

A paranoid man makes paranoid plans.

Post Malone from the song "Paranoid"

Chapter 1

How many of you have recently been ostracized by family members, employers, and long-time friends because of your beliefs about a current topic? How many opportunities have you lost lately because of someone's polarized beliefs about who they think you are? Have you tribalized your associations and the area in which you live? Do you dehumanize others and believe others are doing the same to you? Are you more afraid now than you used to be? In PSYOP, the answers to these questions are called "Impact Indicators." They are used to determine if a PSYOP Campaign is working.

1-9   PSYCHOLOGICAL ACTIONS (PSYACTs)

A Psychological Action (PSYACT) is the occurrence of something that affects the Target Audience. The PSYACT and the responsive behavior create the desired psychological reaction of a Target Audience. It can either be intentionally planned or a natural occurrence. Either way, PSYACTs are implemented (maneuvered) to affect a specific "Target Audience" to support a PSYOP Plan.

1-10   COGNITIVE BATTLESPACE/TERRAIN

Cognitive battlespace/terrain is a war for information, as it is transformed into knowledge via the processes of cognition. The goal is to change the way people think for the purpose of benefiting someone else.

1-11 STATE AND NON-STATE ACTORS

State actors are people who work for a government. Non-state actors do not. However, there are many examples of non-state actors working in direct coordination with state actors to influence Target Audiences in specific ways on behalf of the state. The non-state actors can be non-profit or for-profit entities working on behalf of a state actor to directly influence an individual, a group within a segment of a population, or an entire population of a state (Venezuela), a region (Eastern Europe), or an entire continent (Australia).

> *Non-state actors include non-governmental organizations (NGOs), but equally so multinational corporations, private military organizations, media outlets, terrorist groups, organized ethnic groups, academic institutions, lobby groups, criminal organizations, labor unions or social movements and others.*
> *All wield different forms of power.*
> *Some contribute positively to security and stability whereas others actively undermine it.*
>
> Peter Wijninga, Willem Theo Oosterveld, Jan Hendrik Galdiga & Philipp Marten
> Strategic Monitor 2014: Four Strategic Challenges

Chapter 1

1-12   SHADOW GOVERNMENT(S)

The shadowy government comprises state and non-state actors with clandestine intentions that influence the standing government that is in plain view. They are largely supported by politicians and government agency officials and bureaucrats who've been compromised or indoctrinated first to protect and then to enable a globalist agenda to support the creation of a new world order.

1-13   NATION-STATES

A nation-state is a sovereign territory comprising a culturally homogenous group of individuals who share a common nationalistic identity that supports their way of life based on a system that ensures their continued sovereignty. They share common histories, myths, culture, economy, and legal guidelines. In general discussion, a nation-state is variously called a "country," a "nation," or a "state." But technically, it is a specific form of sovereign state (a political entity on a territory) that is guided by a nation (a cultural entity), and which derives its legitimacy from successfully serving all its citizens.

1-14   MONOLITHIC

A system or structure too large, too regular, or without interesting differences that is unwilling or unable to be changed.

1-15   KARL MARX

Karl Marx (1818–1883) was born in Germany and often treated as a revolutionary, an activist rather than a philosopher, whose works inspired the foundation of many communist regimes in the twentieth century.

1-16   VLADIMIR LENIN

Vladimir Lenin (1870-1924) Russian founder of the Bolsheviks, leader of the Russian Revolution, and first head of the USSR. Under his administration, Russia, and later the Soviet Union, became a one-party socialist state governed by the Communist Party. Ideologically a Marxist, his developments to the ideology are called Leninism.

1-17   JOSEPH STALIN

Joseph Stalin (1878-1953) was born in Georgia, Russian Empire. For a quarter of a century, he dictatorially ruled the Soviet Union and transformed it into a major world power. During the quarter of a century preceding his death, Joseph Stalin probably exercised greater political power than any other figure in history. Stalin industrialized the Union of Soviet Socialist Republics, forcibly collectivized its agriculture, consolidated his position by intensive police terror, helped to defeat Germany, and extended Soviet controls to include a belt of eastern European states. Chief architect of Soviet totalitarianism and a skilled but phenomenally ruthless organizer, he destroyed the remnants of individual freedom and failed to promote individual prosperity, yet he created a mighty military-industrial complex and led the Soviet Union into the nuclear age.

1-18   MAO ZEDONG

Mao Zedong (1893-1976) was born in South Central China. Also known as Chairman Mao, he was a Chinese communist revolutionary who founded the People's Republic of China (PRC), which he led as the chairman of the Chinese Communist Party (CCP) from the establishment of the PRC in

1949 until his death in 1976. Ideologically a Marxist–Leninist, his theories, military strategies, and political policies are collectively known as Maoism.

1-19   MARXIST-LENINIST

The type of Marxism that was developed by Vladimir Lenin before the political changes in Russia in 1917 or someone who follows this. Marxism–Leninism was the official ideology of Joseph Stalin and the former Union of Soviet Socialist Republics (USSR) and by extension of the international communist movement during the twentieth century. The Chinese Communist Party is a variety of Marxism–Leninism that Mao Zedong developed to realize a socialist revolution in the agricultural, pre-industrial society of the Republic of China and later the People's Republic of China. The claim that Mao Zedong had adapted Marxism–Leninism to Chinese conditions evolved into the idea that he had updated it fundamentally, applying it to the world. After the Sino-Soviet split of the 1960s, the Chinese Communist Party and the Communist Party of the Soviet Union each claimed to be the sole heir and successor to Joseph Stalin concerning the correct interpretation of Marxism–Leninism and the ideological leader of communism.

1-20   COMMUNISM

The belief in a society without different social classes, in which the methods of production are owned and controlled by all its members, who work as much as they can and receive what they need, or a social and political system based on this belief. Eric D. Weitz states that the mass killing in communist states is a natural consequence of the failure of the rule of law, commonly seen during periods of social upheaval in the 20th century. For both communist and non-communist mass killings, "genocides occurred at moments of extreme social crisis, often generated by the very policies of the regimes" and are not inevitable but are political decisions. Steven Rosefielde writes that communist rulers had to choose between changing course and "terror-command" and that often, they chose the latter.

1-21   SOCIALISM

The set of beliefs that states that all people are equal and should share equally in a country's money, or the political systems based on these beliefs. In The Road to Serfdom by Friedrich Hayek (written between 1940 and 1943) the Austrian-British economist and philosopher argued that the more even distribution of wealth through the nationalization of the means of production cannot be achieved without a loss of political, economic, and human rights. He argued that, to achieve control over means of production and distribution of wealth; it is necessary for such socialists to acquire significant powers of coercion. Hayek argued that the road to socialism leads society to totalitarianism and argued that fascism and Nazism were the inevitable outcoe of socialist trends in Italy and Germany during the preceding period.

1-22   CAPITALISM

An economic and political system in which property, business, and industry are controlled by private owners rather than by the state, with the purpose of making a profit. French anarchist Pierre-Joseph Proudhon opposed government privilege that protects capitalist banking and land interests and the accumulation or acquisition of property (and any form of coercion that led to it) which he believed hampered competition and kept wealth in the hands of the few. The Spanish individualist anarchist Miguel Giménez Igualada saw that "capitalism is an effect of government; the disappearance of government means capitalism falls from its pedestal vertiginously ... That which we call capitalism is not something else but a product of the State, within which the only thing that is being pushed forward is profit, good or badly acquired. And so to fight against capitalism is a pointless task, since be it State capitalism or Enterprise capitalism, as long as Government exists, exploiting capital will exist. The fight, but of consciousness, is against the State."

Chapter 1

1-23   FASCISM

A nationalistic and anti-Communist system of government like that of Italy (1922-43), where all aspects of society are controlled by the state and all criticism or opposition is suppressed. Fascism is placed on the far-right wing of the political spectrum. Fascism rejects the claims that violence is intrinsically bad and supports imperialism, political violence, and war to support the state's goals. Fascists often advocate for the establishment of one political party and political system that forbids all opposition parties and prohibits opposition of the state and its assertions. It's regarded as the most extreme and complete form of authoritarianism. Fascism opposes Marxism, anarchism, democracy, pluralism, liberalism, socialism and requires extreme control and regulation over public and private life.

1-24   UNIPARTY REPRESENTATIVES

Members of the major political parties who combine into a clandestine alliance. They reserve partial loyalty toward selected causes to advance a country politically along the path of socialism that leads to communism. In socialist countries, the UniParty moves the direction of the country directly toward communism. Members are usually supported passively or actively by foreign state actors or non-state actors who seek a communist global system. The UniParty is classically referred to as the Vanguard Party, and the concept was started by Vladimir Lenin as part of the Russian Revolution of 1917.

1-25   VANGUARD PARTY REPRESENTATIVES

A vanguard party representative is a political party member who knowingly or unknowingly prepares the political environment at the early part of a mass-action political movement and of a revolution. In the habitual or established practice of political science, the concept of the vanguard party is composed of professional revolutionaries who seek the consolidation of political parties into a single political party.

1-26   COUNTRY FIRST REPRESENTATIVES

In whatever country they serve, whatever political system they serve or whatever political party they serve, they support the nation's best practices on behalf of their citizenry and protect the sovereignty of their nation-state. In Nigeria they are known as Nigeria First representatives, in Israel they are considered Israel First representatives and in America they are considered America First representatives, and etc in all other countries. America First representatives should not be confused with any America First political party or the America First Committee (AFC), a special interest group that was started in 1940. The America First Committee had a stance of staying out of WWII, citing the Monroe Doctrine that was against intervention into European affairs and were mired by claims of anti-semitism. However, the AFC was dissolved in 1941 after the attack at Pearl Harbor and they encouraged their 800,000 members to support the war effort. Former U.S. Presidents Gerald Ford, (Republican) and John F. Kennedy (Democrat) were former supporters of the AFC.

The political catch phrase "America First" has been used as a slogan for various political parties and candidates but was originally coined in 1916 by President Woodrow Wilson (Democrat). Today's modern Country First representatives are not an organization, but are all representatives formed across the political spectrum who represent an ideology that supports open debate and the non-violent political will from various in-country political parties to resolve in-state political differences based on the consent of the governed. Where the UniParty chooses to eventually consolidate all political parties into one political party that supports a globalist agenda and the end of nation-states; the Country First representatives desire multiple parties so long as the political party does not support actions that lead to the demise of the nation-state they represent.

Chapter 1

Homework Break

Please consider all the information presented so far, while seeking additional information and using your critical thinking skills to answer these questions. Write your answers on this page.

1. Now that you know the definition of a PSYACT, have you seen one? If so, what happened and how were people affected?

2. What TAs are you a part of? (Consider your gender, age, background, and beliefs) This is how you are assessed for targeted manipulation.

3. How do you avoid being part of a PSYOP?

4. Can you compare and contrast the elements of hybrid, irregular and unrestricted warfare?

5. How is Lenin's Vanguard Party similar to the modern Uniparty?

Chapter 1

6. How is Capitalism destructive to the citizenry and how do we prevent the destructive effects?

7. How is Socialism destructive to the citizenry and how do we prevent the destructive effects?

8. How is Fascism destructive to the citizenry and how do we prevent the destructive effects?

9.   How is Communism destructive to the citizenry and how do we prevent the destructive effects?

10.   What are the main differences between Country First Representatives and UniParty Representatives?

Chapter 1

Chapter 2
The Big Game and a Few of the Players

For we are opposed around the world by a monolithic and ruthless conspiracy that relies primarily on covert means for expanding its sphere of influence... on infiltration instead of invasion, on subversion instead of elections, on intimidation instead of free choice, on guerrillas by night instead of armies by day. It is a system which has conscripted vast human and material resources into the building of a tightly knit, highly efficient machine that combines military, diplomatic, intelligence, economic, scientific and political operations. Its preparations are concealed, not published. Its mistakes are buried, not headlined. Its dissenters are silenced, not praised. No expenditure is questioned, no rumor is printed, no secret is revealed.

President John F. Kennedy | Assassinated American President

2-1   YOUR MISSION – SHOULD YOU CHOOSE TO ACCEPT IT

For the first time in history, there is a global PSYOP agenda to consolidate power using digital platforms to affect everyone on macro and micro levels. The goal is to achieve the borderless consolidation of nations. This is all designed to prepare citizens for centralized control by a globalist elite government superstructure run by the likes of leaders from the World Economic Forum. Meanwhile, as it happens, everyone is addicted to digital dopamine, and their next fix is just a click away.

Rome has become the world. We are Nero, and the fiddle is the latest twerk video on TikTok. You can play the fiddle or save Rome, but you can't do both. Please step away from the apple tree and stop talking to the snake. Resist the contemporary Tower of Babel. Protect your mind – control your emotions.

It is too simplistic to merely classify conflict as 'Big and Conventional' versus 'Small or Irregular.' Today's enemies, and tomorrow's, will employ combinations of warfare types. Non-state actors may mostly employ irregular forms of warfare, but will clearly support, encourage, and participate in conventional conflict if it serves their ends. Similarly, nation-states may well engage in irregular

Chapter 2

conflict in addition to conventional types of warfare to achieve their goals...
Clearly the United States must be prepared for the full spectrum of conflict
from all fronts and realize that preparing our forces for only selected
types of conflict will be a recipe for defeat.

Lieutenant Colonel, Frank Hoffman | U.S. Marines (Retired)
Research Fellow, Center for Emerging Threats and Opportunities (CETO)
at the Potomac Institute for Policy Studies | Author of *Conflict*
in the 21st Century: The Rise of Hybrid Wars

2-2   YOUR NEIGHBOR IS NOT YOUR ENEMY

In 5GW, the real adversary attacks by cornering you into polarized thinking. Your neighbors are most likely not your enemy, but it might feel that way sometimes. Right? The same is happening with them. And I bet it's because of messaging you've both received from an internet source rather than anything you know about each other on a personal level. Stop now, and instead of relying on your emotional responses, follow what you personally know and can logically deduce to be true. All of you. Please.

2-3   AMBIGUITY AND RANDOMNESS

All actions are precipitated by thoughts, attitudes, and decisions, incorrect or otherwise. Mass manipulation requires the use of physical situations which are framed into psychologically focused messages that are repeated over and over from various sources, told in their own way to affect people's attitudes for the purpose of influencing their behavior. Ambiguity and randomness are tenants of 5GW, and that's the reason people can't see the manipulation occurring.

The primary goal is to control people indirectly, since indirect control reduces the chance of rebellion against the controlling group or individual. Overtness exposes the manipulator. Instead, the goal is to control conditions insidiously and use psychologically effective messaging to frame the perspective of a situation. This in turn manipulates the attitudes of the populace and consequently influences their behavior at will.

2-4   AVOID THE SUCK

If done correctly, 5GW causes people to lead themselves in the desired direction so that the manipulator avoids detection. Shadowy governments create funnels that can't be avoided without training. If you get near the opening of the funnel, you will be sucked into its vortex. Then you'll unknowingly succumb to the PSYOP, and you'll be along for the ride with everyone else. After reading this *Citizen's Guide* from cover to cover and sharing the information with others, you will have learned that what appears ambiguous and random is not. This is your training to see behind the curtain and learn how to keep from being sucked into the grey-zone funnel of turmoil.

2-5   YOUR FEAR IS JUSTIFIED

The fear is that a single "Shadow Government" is secretly utilizing the aspects of hybrid, irregular, and unrestricted warfare against us and that we are not smart enough to figure it out. It's not even a question; this is absolutely happening. But the questions remaining are, "Who is responsible?" and "How do we protect ourselves from this shadow government?"

Globally, there are many governments and equally as many shadowy governments leveraging numerous useful idiots and using the conditions of the environment to shape perspectives to achieve their objectives.

The useful idiots, the leftists who idealistically believe in the beauty of the Soviet socialist or Communist or whatever system, when they get disillusioned, they become their worst enemies. That's why my KGB instructors specifically made the point: never bother with leftists. Forget about these political prostitutes. Aim higher. [...] They serve a purpose only at the stage of destabilization of a nation. For example, your leftists in the United States:

Chapter 2

all these professors and all these beautiful civil rights defenders.
They are instrumental in the process of the subversion
only to destabilize a nation. When their job is completed,
they are not needed any more. They know too much.
Some of them, when they get disillusioned, when they see
that Marxist-Leninists come to power—obviously they get offended—
they think that they will come to power. That will never happen,
of course. They will be lined up against the wall and shot.

Yuri Bezmenov | Former Soviet KGB

2-6   TWO-STAGE COMMUNIST REVOLUTION – THE GREAT RESET

Marxist–Leninist revolutionary theory maintains that a two-stage communist revolution is needed to replace capitalism. In a two-stage communist revolution, it starts with capitalism which must be passed through to get to communism via socialism. Socialism is the first stage and communism, the second, thus a two-stage communist revolution. This is the goal for the state and non-state actors working to establish the new world order and the declared "Great Reset" as stated by the World Economic Forum.

The UniParty, knowingly and unknowingly, facilitates this two-stage revolution. UniParty members pretend to be on separate sides of the political spectrum but on the globalist topics they equally support the changes. They disregard nationalistic best practices that would help the citizenry.

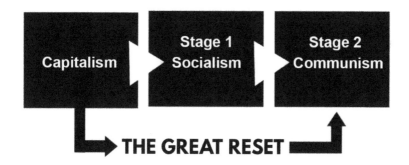

Diagram 2-6
TWO-STAGE COMMUNIST REVOLUTION
The Citizen's Guide to Fifth Generation Warfare

2-7   STUCK IN THE MIDDLE

Contrary to the popular conspiracy theories about a singular shadow government, there is not just one who controls absolutely everything. There are a few shadowy governments, and they use the same tactics and strategies against each other as much as they use them to manage and manipulate the populations within their dominion and control. The people are stuck in the middle.

For now, shadowy government threats to America and most of the world have similar generalized goals, and they collaborate with each other . . . until they don't. There are state actors like the Chinese Communist Party with their alliances such as Venezuela, North Korea, Iran, Russia, and the radicalized parts of the Islamic world, and there are non-state actors, such as organizations and programs funded by the likes of George Soros, Mark Zuckerberg, Bill Gates, the World Economic Forum, the World Trade Organization, and the World Health Organization.

Together, they represent the major individual players and external groups who run networks of shadowy government loyalists. These loyalists then develop and promote conditions to support a globalist agenda for a new world order. Within the United States, there are also threats that support the external groups.

2-8   UNIPARTY LOYALISTS

Domestically, the combination of political parties working in secret is an example of the smaller shadowy government faction at work. They work on behalf of major shadowy government groups rather than the people of their country. Within legitimate governments, internal political party members have surreptitiously combined their efforts to create a globalist-minded UniParty that is willing to forgo the sanctity of its country's values. These UniParties exist in most of the first-world countries of the West and most of Asia. Countries on the African continent and those in Latin America should not be excluded.

The United States, United Kingdom, Australia, Holland, Singapore, and Canada are countries with strong, globalist-minded UniParty factions within their governments. There are others such as Germany, Italy, and Switzerland who also have ever-growing globalist agendas being promoted through UniParty groups.

The 'UniParty' is a term that describes the globalist establishment's control over politics and policy to the extent that every or nearly every major political party or politician are controlled by them and, thus, have far more in common than differences, policy-wise. It is essentially synonymous with the deep state, as it retains control almost regardless of which political party or politician is elected. An example is the general movement by both the Republican and Democratic parties in the United States to continually expand the size and reach of the Federal government into every area of one's life, the only significant difference being whether the apparatus should be run by unionized government employees (the Democrat party approach) or private-sector contractors (the Republican party approach). The UniParty should not be confused with bipartisanship, as the latter views working together as a means to an end, while the UniParty sees different political parties working together as the end in-and-of itself... The UniParty consistently advocates for a net increase in federal spending without any effort to reduce unnecessary social or defense spending, and both parties have a record of supporting gun control. Marxist ideas have "infiltrated" both the Democrat and

Chapter 2

Republican parties... While the traditional mainstream
conservative and liberal parties joined together to govern,
they've agreed on many agenda items,
particularly in advancing big government globalist
policies. The same critics also point out the GOP
(Republican) establishment's readiness to compromise
and back down from their stated positions
as an example of the UniParty.
CONSERVAPEDIA

Chapter 2

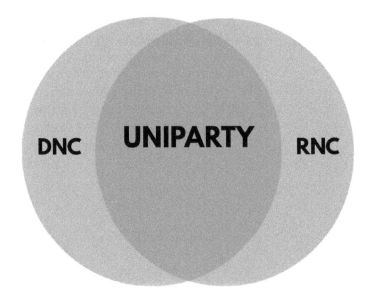

Diagram 2-8
THE UNIPARTY LOYALIST
The Citizen's Guide to Fifth Generation Warfare

Chapter 2

2-9   AMERICA FIRST REPRESENTATIVES – DEFINED
(COUNTRY FIRST REPRESENTATIVES IN NON-AMERICAN COUNTRIES)

Any Democrat, Republican, or other political party member who is not financed by the two major political parties, foreign state actors, or globalist non-state actors. America First Democrats and America First Republicans are identified as such by their pro-alignment with the following:

1. Election integrity
2. Border security
3. Parental rights
4. Medical freedom
5. Bill of Rights
6. Defund UniParty Members and remove them with a fair election process

Funding for the UniParty comes from individual contributions by people like you and corporate contributors funded through profits that are knowingly and unknowingly attained from people also just like us. Why are America First candidates not receiving the funds they should and the UniParty has coffers full of cash? Can you see how your method of consumerism, individual campaign contributions and charitable contributions are financing the communist revolution in your country? All these money transactions are siphoned into funds that support the eventual demise of nation-states. It's all a game based on monetizing your habits and using the monetization to support the globalist agenda. Can you break a habit, or do you want to help your opponent win? How many small businesses were forced out of business during the pandemic lock-downs and how much of that business was absorbed by large corporations that make sizable contributions to political entities and causes? And it's all supported by big tech and weaponized media. Can you see how the game is played? You have more control than you think you do. But can you adjust your life when your desire for convenience and comfort is their weapon? In most cases, we can all buy locally from vetted businesses and it helps our neighbors. And in all cases, we can stop our contributions to UniParty members.

An America First political representative must denounce being a UniParty Member by declining contributions and assistance from the UniParty and their contributors. The UniParty is secretly a vanguard party established to usher in a Marxist-Leninist state. This comes directly from their doctrine, and they are preparing to seize power and establish a one-party socialist

Chapter 2

state through political warfare. In a Marxist–Leninist government, the government controls the means of production and its labor, and it suppresses opposition and counter-revolution with the methods described in this *Guide,* while paving the way for an eventual communist society that is classless and stateless.

The UniParty is secretly a vanguard party established to usher-in a global Marxist-Leninist government. This is from their doctrine, and they are preparing to seize power and establish a one-party socialist state through political warfare. In a Marxist–Leninist government, the government controls the means of production and its labor, suppresses opposition and counter-revolution with the methods described in this guide while paving the way for an eventual communist society that is classless and stateless.

2-10   VANGUARD PARTY TECHNIQUE

A vanguard party is a political party designed to prepare the political environment at the early part of a mass-action political movement and of a revolution. In the habitual or established practice of political science, the concept of the vanguard party is composed of professional revolutionaries. In the United States and other freedom-loving countries, members of a similar vanguard party are cloaked in the legitimate government as UniParty representatives and are supported by a media apparatus. Online "Fact Checkers" often support their actions and provide the appearance of legitimacy

2-11   IT'S A BIG CLUB AND YOU AIN'T IN IT

Typically, the Chinese Communist Party influences world leaders through the World Economic Forum, World Trade Organization, and World Health Organization policies at the global level. The Chinese Communist Party works with organizations funded by George Soros, Bill Gates, and Mark Zuckerberg. Together they manipulate national governments by influencing the top executive leadership appointed by the President of the United States and by replacing them with evermore communistic players. Each person creates a nudge toward the new normal. Then all are replaced by a successor who is more extreme than the last. This process is in continuous development. It occurs insidiously, bit-by-bit, and few notice the succession of subtle changes until it's too late. We must stop this type of continual degradation immediately and push back against their "new normal" campaigns.

The President and other officials at the state, county, and municipal levels such as Senators, Congressional Representatives, States Attorneys

General, Secretaries of State, County Commissioners, District Attorneys, County School Boards, Board of Election Supervisors, and even a select set of Judges are supported through election fraud, large economic enticements, and opportunities that support UniParty members throughout the entire fabric of government.

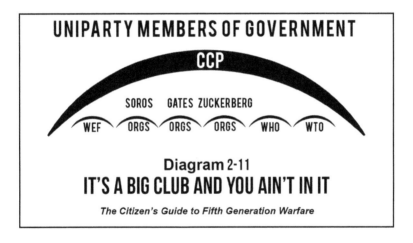

UNIPARTY MEMBERS OF GOVERNMENT

CCP

SOROS   GATES ZUCKERBERG

WEF   ORGS   ORGS   ORGS   WHO   WTO

Diagram 2-11
IT'S A BIG CLUB AND YOU AIN'T IN IT

The Citizen's Guide to Fifth Generation Warfare

Honest minded America First candidates rarely have enough money to compete against UniParty candidates. And the financial elite, who could support the honest candidates, are typically unconcerned parties who have been compromised by corruption of one kind or another.

America's separation from the King of England's control was no different in that there was no financial backing to fight "tyranny" until the financial elite had their profits threatened. They didn't have the political representation to change the situation, so they financed a revolution. In today's world, the financial elite have unlimited access to political representation, regardless of the political ideology of their country, but you don't. Right? So, who is left to finance a revolution? Nobody.

Capitalism, colonialism, socialism, communism, fascism, anarchy, and at least twenty other forms of government all feed from the flesh of their citizenry in one way or another. Some are more brutal than others, while others are more advantageous, but all have a financial elite that doesn't feel the pain you do. Most of the financial elite will continue to support the UniParty until it becomes financially beneficial for them to do something differently. Similarly, the citizenry of all nations will continue to live as they do until they make a plan that's more beneficial and execute it based on the information located in sections: 2-9, 3-1, 7-1, 7-2, 8-3, and 9-11.

Chapter 2

2-12   THE TANGLED WEB THEY WEAVE

Many conservative and liberal lawmakers and political appointees of all political affiliations support the leftist push for abolishing national identity and the nation-state by joining to advance and maintain open border policies. Members of select political parties publicly appear to be on different sides of the political spectrum, but they are motivated by a united globalist agenda. From this they profit personally, and they believe their higher calling is global. In truth, they are puppets to the puppet masters, who possess both seen and unseen dangerous but powerful and uncompromising leverage and influence.

The rumors of an Illuminati, New World Order, Cabal, and the like have always existed and will continue so long as there are elitist people and elitist groups with political, economic, military, and media leverage who want to rule the world. Admittedly, some stories of "Shadow Governments" are beyond fictitious and are sensationalized to the point of fantasy. But don't be fooled. Whether they're called the Deep State in our time or Illuminati in the fantastical past, there is always a pecking order. And someone somewhere will go to extreme lengths to get to the very top of it.

America has seen the collaborative effort of the UniParty and their shadowy government counterparts attack U.S. President Donald J. Trump and his family and business interests, his first National Security Advisor, Lieutenant General (Retired) Michael Flynn and his family, and many others who fought back against the elite takeover of America and who defended America's national sovereignty. These corrupt strategies are not reserved for conservative candidates. According to the (former) Chairwoman of the Democratic National Committee, Donna Brazile, the 2016 Democratic presidential nomination for Bernie Sanders was "rigged" to go to Hillary Clinton. A lot of Americans agree. The Democratic National Committee (DNC) and the Republican National Committee (RNC) are both corrupt. They should be defunded and replaced by political organizations that support the will of the people. The 2016 Presidential ticket would have been Sanders versus Trump had the corruption not existed.

The UniParty of the United States has weaponized the United States Department of Justice as its agent for this radical change. The Internal Revenue Service through the United States Treasury Department is soon to be weaponized against the American people. Similar tactics are happening worldwide in other nations against political figures who don't support the globalist agenda ahead of nationalistic needs. In Italy, the first female Prime Minister, Giorgia Meloni, has been attacked in the

Chapter 2

same way for her Italy-First agenda.

2-13   SOCIAL MEDIA AND INFORMATION FEEDBACK LOOPS

Since the advent of the internet and social media, shadowy governments operating in the grey zone and leveraging the tenets of 5GW have methodically cultivated a bottom-to-top strategy to influence the masses. Prior to the internet and specifically, the rise of social media, there were dishonest lawmakers, traditional media, popular influencers of groups, the movie industry, and leaders across academia who participated in the manipulation and control of the masses. Now, with the internet and its ability to manipulate with bots and social media swarms of digital cry-bullies and censorship, shadowy governments use an unseen hand to manipulate political, societal, and economic change directly through the masses by censoring the messages and influencers they don't want and giving greater access to the messages and influencers that support their agenda.

> *We'll need to mockup fake videos of our own, populate the web*
> *with obvious frauds, to make all versions suspect.*
> Vincent H. O'Neil | Author of *A Pause in the Perpetual Rotation*

Chapter 2

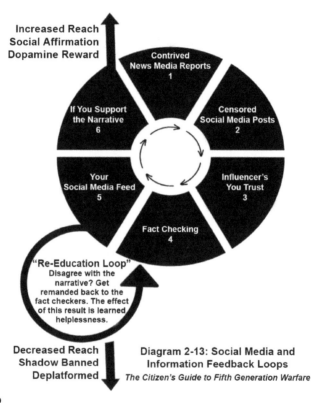

Increased Reach
Social Affirmation
Dopamine Reward

Contrived
News Media Reports
1

If You Support
the Narrative
6

Censored
Social Media Posts
2

Your
Social Media Feed
5

Influencer's
You Trust
3

Fact Checking
4

"Re-Education Loop"
Disagree with the
narrative? Get
remanded back to the
fact checkers. The effect
of this result is learned
helplessness.

Decreased Reach
Shadow Banned
Deplatformed

Diagram 2-13: Social Media and
Information Feedback Loops
The Citizen's Guide to Fifth Generation Warfare

Chapter 2

2-14   SEE A CAT – PAINT A TIGER

The unseen hand controls the populace by making small, controlled groups appear to be a majority audience of a nation who collectively demand change based on the desire of "most" people who remain unaware that they are being manipulated. They are not the majority but have the appearance of the majority because the real majority audience is shadow banned, de-platformed, outright canceled, or swarmed with dissenting programmed bots. Lawmakers, Big Tech, and media react in-kind, touting that they are "with the people" when they support the small groups who have been cloaked as the majority, though they are not.

2-15   WEAPONIZING HUMAN NATURE

Social conformity and confirmation bias are part of human nature. Social conformity is a type of social influence involving a change in belief or behavior to fit in with a group. Confirmation bias is the natural tendency to process information by looking for, or interpreting, information that is consistent with one's existing beliefs.

Both are easily weaponized in the cognitive battlespace of a nation by developing and exploiting polarizing topics that possess a high degree of emotionality. Social conformity is weaponized by showing the small, controlled group(s) as having the "righteous" position; therefore, any opposition is illegitimate and unrighteous. Confirmation bias augments the process. The process for weaponizing these two factors of human nature take a systematic approach.

1.   Discreetly manipulate the smaller group(s) and make them vocal to appear as if they are the majority audience who expresses the needs and desires of the majority.

2.   Leverage messaging and PSYACTs to develop an in-group (us) versus out-group (them) dynamic to recruit the wider audience who desires to simply be the in-group.

3.   Repeat the process to augment the effects and continually demonize the opposition's viewpoints to make them appear as the reviled out-group.

The innate propensity of the human brain to divide the world into us and them valence categories, where the exact membership of the in-group and out-group are socially contingent (hence vulnerable to the

Chapter 2

instruments of propaganda), and the intensity exists along a spectrum from mild to complete dehumanization of the 'othered' group.

Dr. Robert Sapolsky | American Neuroendocrinology Researcher &
Author of *Behave: The Biology of Humans at Our Best and Worst*

2-16   PSYOP IS WEAPONIZED SOCIOLOGY

The in-group reinforces its concepts, values, and motivations through an effective information feedback loop comprised of contrived media reports, social media sharing, and groupthink. While groupthink can generate consensus, it is a negative phenomenon that results in faulty or uninformed thinking and decision-making. The in-group's feedback loop is a media-based sensory prison that looks like a resort, with a staff continually taking every opportunity to affirm the identity of in-group members.

For the out-group, the feedback loop is filled with doubt. The out-group is silenced in secret and publicly demonized to deter the organizing and eventual mobilization of the actual majority audience. Currently, the out-group is the majority audience who is named, blamed, and shamed into obscurity. It is all designed to appear random and organic; far from it, this weaponization is very intentional.

Make the lie big, make it simple, keep saying it,
and eventually they will believe it.

Joseph Goebbels | German Nazi Politician and Propaganda Minister

2-17   PSYCHOGRAPHICS

Psychographics is a clever use of detailed personal data to manipulate people based on their vulnerabilities, deepest desires, and personal history. Psychographics are applied to the study of cognitive attributes such as opinions, interests, attitudes, fears, and beliefs, as well as the study of overt behavior as an individual or as part of a group. They are used to develop a PSYOP plan.

According to *U.S. Army Psychological Operations Process, Tactics, Techniques, and Procedures Manual FM 3-05.301,* psychographics include the following:

- Fears: What does the Target Audience (TA) fear?
- Hates: What does the TA hate?
- Anger: What angers the TA?
- Loves: What does the TA love?
- Shame or embarrassment: What does the TA consider

Chapter 2

shameful or embarrassing?
- What is the TA dissatisfied with? (What are its gripes?)
- What are the cultural norms? (How is the TA expected to act?)
- What does the TA value? (What is important to the TA?)
- What are the frustrations? (What does the TA want that it cannot get?)

2-18   CYBERWARFARE TO IDENTIFY A TARGET AUDIENCE [EXAMPLE]

On October 4, 2022, the Los Angeles District Attorney made an official statement regarding a "cyber intrusion." Eugene Yu, the 51-year-old Chinese-born CEO of Konnech, an election software company, was arrested on suspicion of theft of personal information and computer hard drives. Mr. Yu was required to store data only in the United States with accessibility only to citizens and permanent residents in the United States. Instead, he stored the personal information of election poll workers on servers in China. Based on the info provided in this *Guide*, you can see how hacking the election is as easy as having access to a TA and using the psychographics of the election poll workers to manipulate them.

STATEMENT ON HEAD OF ELECTION WORKER MANAGEMENT COMPANY ARRESTED IN CONNECTION WITH THEFT OF PERSONAL DATA

"I want to thank my prosecutors and investigators for their commitment to eliminating cyber intrusions against government entities and local businesses. Data breaches are an ongoing threat to our digital way of life. When we entrust a company to hold our confidential data, they must be willing and able to protect our personal identifying information from theft. Otherwise, we are all victims. This investigation is concerned solely with the personal identifying information of election workers. In this case, the alleged conduct had no impact on the tabulation of votes and did not alter election results. But security in all aspects of any election is essential so that we all have full faith in the integrity of the election process."

DISTRICT ATTORNEY GEORGE GASCON
October 4, 2022

District Attorney Gascon claims the election was not breached. However, unless he's been able to verify there was no influence campaign focused on the collected information in China, he can't be sure. And how could anyone know for sure? What we do know is that, Eugene Yu, a Chinese-born man, gave the personal details of election poll workers to the CCP. Whether Yu was involved or not, he gave them access. We'll leave

Chapter 2

the determination of what occurred to your intellect and critical thinking.

2-19   PRIMARY INFLUENCE TACTICS

The next segment is listed with the military examples U.S. Army manual referenced in 2-17. As you read the primary influence tactics, ask yourself if you have seen these used on the citizenry recently. Imagine other examples as you read the military examples from the list below. Primary influence tactics are based on psychographics and widely apply to many situations, cultures, and TAs. By using the appropriate influence tactics in PSYOP products and PSYACTs, the persuasiveness of PSYOP will be magnified. The following are military examples of primary influence tactics:

Rewards and punishments: If you do X, you will get Y, or if you do not do X and then Y will happen to you. "Example: "Surrender, and you will be treated well; continue to fight, and you will be killed."

Expertise: Speakers of authority on a subject, tell you that rewards/ punishments will occur if you do or do not do X. Example: "Oil Minister Gregor (a key communicator/alleged expert on the subject) states that if rebel groups continue to sabotage oil pipelines, the national economy will be seriously affected."

Gifts: Giving something as a gift before requesting compliance. The idea is that the target will feel the need to reciprocate later. Example: "This well and cistern are a gift to the people of Birmingville from the coalition forces...demonstration of our good will and hope for mutual cooperation in the future."

Debt: Calling in past favors. Example: "Coalition forces have done a lot for Birmingville, Elder Chang: the new school, the well in the center of town... these insurgents are endangering all we have worked for together. We need your help in stopping these groups by reporting any information you and your people may discover."

Aversive stimulation: Continuous punishment, and the cessation of punishment, is contingent on compliance. Example: "We will continue to bomb your position unless you surrender immediately."

Moral appeal: Entails finding moral common ground, and then using the moral commitments of a person to obtain compliance. Example: "The killing of innocent civilians is wrong; please help the security forces stop this tragic loss of innocent life by reporting any information on terrorist activities."

Positive and negative self-feeling: You will feel better/bad if you do X.

Chapter 2

Example: "Become part of something bigger than yourself, know honor and take pride in your work...join the national security forces!"

Positive and negative altercasting: Good people do X / Bad people do Y. Example: "Red Tribe members are brave and honorable people who care about the future of their country and are not intimidated by rebel groups. Call and report insurgent activity now on the coalition hotline."

Positive and negative esteem of others: Other people will think highly/ less of you if you do X. Example: "Earn the respect of your friends and the pride of your family...join the Patriotsville National Guard now!"

Fear: Bad things will happen to you if you do X. Example: "Only death and fire await those who continue to fight...surrender now."

If a period of peace can be used to soften up a future enemy, the totalitarian armies may be able in time of war to win a cheap and easy victory. Totalitarian psycholog- ical warfare is directed largely toward this end. It is an effort to propagandize and hypnotize the world into submission.

Joost A.M. Meerloo | Author of *The Rape of the Mind: The Psychology of Thought Control, Menticide, and Brainwashing*

Chapter 2

2-20   PROTECT YOUR MIND – CONTROL YOUR EMOTIONS

PSYOP is only one aspect of 5GW. PSYOP is the underlying non-kinetic (non-violent) part of hybrid, irregular, and unrestricted warfare. Though it is non-kinetic in nature, PSYOP can have kinetic (violent) effects. A PSYOP campaign might induce a riot. The PSYOP campaign is not violent, but the riot might be. PSYOP is not new, but now, anyone can have access to your mind through social media, which is contrived for political purposes. Everything is weaponized until something better can be weaponized. You should protect your mind and control your emotions, or your mind will become their weapon.

No more war pigs have the power.
Hand of God has struck the hour.

Black Sabbath | From the Song "War Pigs"

Chapter 2
Homework Break

Please consider all the information presented so far, while seeking additional information and using your critical thinking skills to answer these questions. Write your answers on this page.

1. Define: Fifth Column

2. Define: Scapegoating

3.   How does the UniParty function as the action-arm of state and non-state actors during a political warfare campaign?

4.   Is today's internet censorship the same as burning books in past years? If so, who burned the books and why?

5.   List two (2) primary influence tactics you've seen the government use on the citizenry.

Chapter 2

6.　　What is the purpose of using psychographics to refine messaging?

Chapter 3
Make Ready

'This is a developing definition,' Murray cautioned.
'But right now, [decision dominance] is the ability for a commander to sense,
understand, decide, act, and assess faster and more effectively than any adversary.'

General John "Mike" Murray | U.S. Army Futures Command

3-1   BATTLEFIELD PREPARATION

Your mind in 5GW is the cognitive battlespace where shadowy
governments aim to achieve decision dominance. The critical nature of
defense of your mind at the individual level cannot be understated.

3-2   MANIPULATION AND DECISION DOMINANCE

Decision dominance in the cognitive battlespace of a nation means
achieving a reasonable amount of predictability to anticipate how people
will react to a situation or circumstance and then leveraging PSYACT(s) to
facilitate the desired behavior of a target audience to support the PSYOP
plan. A PSYACT is the occurrence of something that affects the Target

Audience. If the PSYACT and the responsive behavior create the desired effects more efficiently than the opposition's PSYACTs and PSYOP plan, then decision dominance in the cognitive battlespace is likely to have been achieved by the more effective opponent.

PSYACTs are only limited by the imagination of the people conducting the PSYOP based on existing usable conditions of the environment. In PSYOP, if a situation exists or appears to exist, it's usable. PSYACTs amplify the PSYOP plan. In today's environment, everything from the threat of a nuclear strike to the restriction of energy resources are PSYACTs that manipulate behavior based on some level of decision dominance. Whether or not the literal acts are carried out, the PSYACT will intentionally affect how the TA views the situation.

In the event of an actual nuclear strike, expect disinformation to amplify the overall damage as part of a co-existing PSYOP plan from the attacker, and whoever is attacked will do the same, along with their allies. The anxiety among all TAs involved will be internationally destabilizing and personally overwhelming. Decision dominance will ultimately determine who the winner of the most effective PSYOP plan will be.

Chapter 3

3-3   HOW TO MAKE PEOPLE KILL PEOPLE

Influencing people to kill others happens in four phases:

1. Polarization
2. Tribalization
3. Dehumanization
4. Killing

Diagram 3-3
HOW TO MAKE PEOPLE KILL PEOPLE
The Citizen's Guide to Fifth Generation Warfare

3-4   POLARIZATION

The path to destruction is sadly very simple to manipulate when PSYOP is applied, and it starts with a polarization phase. Polarized thinking in 5GW is the manufactured sense of life-or-death using messages, videos, or memes. In the future other techniques will be used. If a PSYOP campaign tricks your emotions enough to polarize your thinking, physiologically your adrenal glands trigger your mind into an extreme response. The campaign locks you into a rigid way of thinking because you feel it will keep you safe. It invokes a sense of commitment to a cause or outcome.

PSYOP campaigns trigger the natural physiological "fight or flight" response to claim your mind and affect your attitude toward a situation or circumstance. From that point forward, people will only be able to accept ideas and concepts that confirm their bias. Anything else will feel threatening and will be rejected. Next in this path to destruction comes the tribalization phase.

3-5   TRIBALIZATION

Tribalization is an act of self-segregation with a group. How many people do you know who are tribalizing? Maybe they quit their job and want to collaborate with people who are more like them, or maybe they moved to another neighborhood, even another state. The moment you identify yourself with a group, whether by wearing a sports jersey of your favorite team, a hat that identifies your political views, or a military or paramilitary uniform, you've tribalized yourself on some level.

Some tribalization is harmless. For example, wearing a football jersey in America and sitting in the stands with other people that support the same team on game day is relatively harmless. Yet even that has been known to get out-of-hand in the parking lot before or after a game, especially if some loudmouths are tossing back too many drinks. It's easy for it all to go too far.

Other forms of tribalization include religious and political ideologies. It seems that, in today's world, politics has become people's religion, and their favorite news station has become their church. Historically, this type of tribalization comes with a high degree of prolonged emotionality and can easily lead to intentionally planned bloodshed. Because of the PSYOP in this fifth generation of war, some people are now tribalizing in ways to isolate themselves from their biological families, claiming it's a necessary evil to save the world. America has not seen this type of tribalization since the civil war, where brother fought brother in the

Chapter 3

battles between the north and south.

In the past when someone was abducted by a cult, one of the warning signs that it was a cult was how it isolated them from their family and friends. Nowadays, people are doing it to themselves based on PSYOP campaigns that they don't see and wouldn't acknowledge if they did. They are making their own cults and are self-radicalized based on their susceptibilities. The unseen hand of a PSYOP campaign is making them feel vulnerable through messaging. Tribalization is a major factor in the effectiveness of 5GW and is potentially a contributing factor for civil war.

3-6   DEHUMANIZATION

The tribalization phase shapes the conditions for the dehumanization phase. In the dehumanization phase, people feel their tribe is the only tribe that deserves to live. All the other tribes are responsible for the destruction of the world; so, they must die or join the "right" tribe to ensure the survival of themselves and the future of those they love. Once we get into the dehumanization phase, if it continues, only killing comes next. You are being cognitively prepared to isolate and feel demonized by each other for the purpose of killing one another to divide the country and usher in a new political establishment.

3-7   IT'S NOT TOO LATE TO RESIST

This strategy is not new (it has been present during other generations of war), but in 5GW it's the primary focus rather than an ancillary and supporting technique. Nobody has a monopoly on these techniques, nor are they specific to one group. The process never changes, and everybody does it. Adolf Hitler used this strategy on the Jews, just as Andrew Jackson did on the indigenous peoples of North America, and Joseph Stalin did on the people of Ukraine. Academia does it when they preach anti-nationalistic rhetoric. The Hutu did it against the Tutsi in Rwanda. ANTIFA does it against symbols of authority, and MAGA extremists do it to resist the most innocuous of ideas for change. In just the same way, Mao Zedong dehumanized and killed at least 45 million of his own people between 1958 and 1962.

The same mental process is how Warfighters of all nations mentally prepare for war. We polarize our thinking to develop a sense of righteousness and selflessness to perform in a lethal environment; we tribalize by being part of a military unit that wears a uniform and suffers or succeeds together; we dehumanize our enemy so that they are easy to kill justifiably on the battlefield as we accomplish our mission for the greater good.

Chapter 3

This is always the process, and now it's unknowingly happening in the digital space to manipulate civilian societies worldwide. In no way is it based on the consent of the governed or the will of the people. It's based solely on those who want to manipulate all of us to give up the sanctity of our country's values and turn toward a global agenda. Do not be fooled.

3-8 AGENTS OF ACTION: TWO TYPES

Agents of action create PSYACTs (Psychological Actions) both purposely and inadvertently. These agents are either discretionary or incidental agents of action. The discretionary agents of action do so intentionally with the expressed intent of augmenting the PSYOP plan. Incidental agents of action aren't primarily attempting to further the PSYOP plan, but something they do inadvertently creates an additional usable opportunity.

In the context of shadowy governments or Deep State operatives, the discretionary agent of action is intentionally part of the plan, and the incidental agent of action unintentionally creates a target of opportunity secondary to whatever the initial action was. PSYOP incorporates the purposeful, accidental, and unintentional actions of others.

3-9   DISCRETIONARY AGENTS OF ACTION [EXAMPLE]

During the war in Sadr City, Iraq, the Coalition Forces fought the Iranian-backed Mehdi Militia. The American tactical PSYOP team in Sadr City had identified liberal young females as a TA that would report militia activity and started a successful campaign that included a secret tip-line.

The Mehdi Militia's main enforcer was a man named Abu D'ua (Dura) who ran the special activities section for Muqtada al Sadr, known as the Punishment Committee. One night, he killed two young Iraqi girls on a street corner where sheep were routinely slaughtered, and he did it in front of a crowd. The girls were both shot in the head. One had the muzzle of an AK-47 pressed against her vagina, and she was shot.

Following the murders, several notes were left on the bodies for Americans to find, claiming the girls were spies and prostitutes for Americans. Both girls appeared to be under the age of sixteen, and neither was a spy or prostitute. They were sacrificed to manipulate the people of Sadr City.

This was a PSYACT to enhance a PSYOP plan to control the populace, and Abu D'ua was the discretionary agent of action for the militia. The location was intentional, the defilement of one victim's female anatomy was intentional, the notes were intentional, and the time of night it occurred was intentional.

The intent of this PSYACT was to influence fathers and mothers to keep their teenage female family members away from American soldiers and prevent them from reporting on Mehdi Militia activity. It was also done to demoralize the American tactical PSYOP team that developed the campaign. This is a brutal example of how extreme a PSYACT can be and what a discretionary agent of action is.

On the following page is a photo of Abu D'ua (Dura), Discretionary Agent of Action for the Mehdi Militia, and one of the blood-soaked notes left on one of the girl's bodies claiming the young girls were prostitutes for Americans.

3-10   INCIDENTAL AGENTS OF ACTION - [EXAMPLE]

If a novice firearms owner were to be at home cleaning his firearm, and he negligently failed to unload and clear the weapon properly prior to cleaning it, and if, due to his negligence, he accidentally shot his infant child, it would be a tragic mishap. However, the media and the UniParty members could spin the situation into an argument for more gun laws. In this incident, the unfortunate shooting is a PSYACT and the person who fired the weapon would be an incidental agent of action.

Chapter 3

All PSYACTs are performed by either a discretionary agent of action (done at their will for their intended purpose) or an incidental agent of action, whose actions are used to support a PSYOP plan secondary to an occurrence that agent caused.

3-11   THEY WALK AMONG US

Think to yourself of a time when you saw something tragic or spectacular on the news that got spun into a national uproar because the media chose to report on selective information that caused a high degree of emotionality from the public. Selective information is used in media to frame a situation to cause a specific psychological effect. Whoever caused the event could be either a discretionary or an incidental agent of action. Sometimes we don't know. The media can also be a discretionary agent of action. The poor souls involved in a tragic event can be considered unwitting incidental agents of action.

From now on, when you see something in the media presented with selective information that gets emotionally spun into a national uproar, you will know you are seeing a PSYACT that involves discretionary and incidental agents of action to augment a PSYOP plan. In 5GW, PSYACTs are performed by agents of action, discretionary and incidental, including but not limited to:

- Terrorists
- Traditional media broadcasters
- Podcasters
- Criminals
- Musical artists
- Religious leaders
- Social Media influencers of any kind
- Social media content creators
- Lawmakers
- Hackers
- Journalists
- Meme makers
- Video producers
- Movie makers
- Social Justice advocates
- Street artists (i.e., Banksy)
- Law Enforcement agencies
- Government agencies
- Non-Government agencies
- ...and you

Chapter 3

3-12   LITHUANIA EMPOWERED THEIR CITIZENS

In 2015, while the Russian military was on the march in Europe, Lithuania armed its citizens with the information they needed to have a standing insurgency ready the moment Russia's troops crossed their border. They took a position of unity against their enemy. That wasn't the first time such strategies were put into play, and it won't be the last. Arm yourselves against shadowy government strategies.

Manual On What to Do in Case of War Distributed to Lithuanian Schools

Some 2,000 copies of 'What Should We Know About Preparations for Extreme Situations and War' were handed over to the Education Supply Centre on Wednesday. The centre will deliver them to school libraries.

Marius Jatautas, director of the Mobilization and Civil Resistance Department, says the publications will reach all schools in 60 municipalities.

'Across Lithuania, all schools will receive them 100 percent, as the Mobilization Department is responsible for mobilizing all municipalities,' Jatautas told journalists.

Chapter 3

In his words, Lithuania should prepare for possible foreign aggression after the developments in Ukraine, as the 'security situation is very fragile'.

'The whole world was living in a dream that war was not possible....' Jatautas said.

Viktoras Blinovas, director of the Baltupiai progymnasium in Vilnius, said the publication will benefit schools.

'It seems to me that the book and its content will benefit adults, teachers, school principals, as we are responsible for health and lives of children at the times they are in school. [...] Therefore, we have to be ready for unexpected cases of threat to children, teachers and the society,' Blinovas said.

The 98-page book contains scores of practical advice, starting with equipping a shelter in the basement to advise on what people should do in case of explosion or if they are taken hostage. 'Don't panic and stay calm. Shots fired outside the window is not the end of the world,' reads the book.

Chapter 3

In case of a war, civilian residents are advised to evacuate or purchase a weapon for self-defence, if evacuation is impossible.

Defence Minister Juozas Olekas told BNS that 'the book satisfies the needs of people who, after the Russian aggression in Ukraine, started inquiring about what they should do in case of similar developments in Lithuania.'

BNS | The Lithuania Tribune

Chapter 3

Homework Break

Please consider all the information presented so far, while seeking additional information and using your critical thinking skills to answer these questions. Write your answers on this page.

1.   What is the difference between Discretionary and Incidental agents of action?

2.   Why and how is selective information used in the media?

Chapter 3

3.   What is decision dominance?

4.   Why is polarization a positive trait for members of the military but not a positive trait for the citizenry in our time?

5.   How have news stations become churches?

6.   Define gaslighting.

Chapter 4

Know Your Physical and Cognitive Environment

Activities conducted to enable a resistance movement or insurgency to coerce, disrupt, or overthrow a government or occupying power by operating through or with an underground, auxiliary, and guerrilla force in a denied area.

Department of Defense Dictionary of Military Terms (Joint Pub 1-02) | The current definition of Unconventional Warfare, approved by the U.S. Special Operations Command (2009)

4-1   DENIED AREA

The United States Department of Defense defines a denied area as "an area under enemy or unfriendly control in which friendly forces cannot expect to operate successfully within existing operational constraints and force capabilities." To the enemies of the United States, the United States is a denied area to them, and they cannot conduct conventional military operations inside the denied area to overthrow our government by force. They must use unconventional tactics and irregular strategies to achieve their goals.

4-2   UNDERGROUND

According to "Human Factors Considerations of Undergrounds in Insurgencies" by United States Army Special Operations Command and The John Hopkins University Applied Physics Laboratory National Security Analysis Department, an Underground is "a clandestine organization established to operate in areas denied to the armed or public components or conduct operations not suitable for the armed or public components."

"Globalization has also changed underground operations in numerous ways. Insurgencies, enabled by low-cost transportation, Internet based technologies, and other information technologies, can more easily recruit, communicate, and operate across borders."

4-3   AUXILIARY

According to the same publication listed directly in 4-1, Auxiliary is "the support element of the irregular organization whose organization and operations are clandestine in nature and whose members do not openly indicate their sympathy or involvement with the irregular movement. Members of the auxiliary are more likely to be occasional participants of the insurgency with full-time occupations."

4-4   WE ARE AT WAR

Look around the world you live in. Now that you know what to look for, can you see members of the Underground and Auxiliary who are working in the Denied Area of your country? Do you see a UniParty supporting the globalist agenda of state and non-state actors? And can you see how PSYOP works? Can you think of any PSYACTs you might have seen lately? Do you understand why people can't see what's happening and why they couldn't accept it even if they did?

If so, you are beginning to understand 5GW. This is what the fifth generation of war looks like. We are absolutely at war with an enemy who seeks to subjugate you and your family for the foreseeable future. Accept it and don't be paralyzed by fear. If you don't act, what do you think will happen?

4-5   HOW SOME PEOPLE ARE RECRUITED

Underground operations in 5GW have never been easier, for many reasons. One reason is the use of social media to locate a TA who is empathetic to a particular cause. Second, the ease of recruitment for fundraising, labor, or new active members is as easy as tracking down people who use hashtags. Hashtags connect people together who are willing to express their sentiments. If someone uses the hashtag #DefundThePolice, then it's very easy to identify that person as someone who is susceptible to motivations that are against the police.

The hashtag #ComeAndTakeIt will provide a list of people who are pro-gun. Hashtags provide a way for people to self-identify as a TA and be cultivated. From that point, they can be assessed for a myriad of reasons, and this important assessment phase can be done from anywhere in the world by an unknown entity. Following a hashtag simply by clicking on it and seeing who else is using it leads to social media profiles that are full of personal information. In short order, the people with the profiles can be assessed for the best way to manipulate them based on the personal information they've made publicly available. If it's a middle-aged woman who spends a lot of time online and has a deceased son who she appears to mourn while sitting in a large home in Beverly Hills, California, one might assume she has money and a soft spot for men who remind her of her son. Those vulnerabilities can be assessed and exploited.

If it's a young girl who appears politically disenfranchised, comes from a broken family, and mentions needing better psych meds, her vulnerabilities can be assessed, and a manipulative person can be put in place to make contact, recruit her, and bring her into a group to provide her a renewed sense of identity and purpose in life with people who value her. Then she can be used to recruit the males she knows, or she can be encouraged to run for political office.

For the novice, these techniques can find people one at a time, but for the professional, they can be done en masse with commercially available computer programs that retrieve information from the internet and aggregate it through processes called social media scraping and web crawling. Web crawling and scraping social media data can be done in real time (and very rapidly).

Such data can come from diverse sources such as Twitter, LinkedIn groups, blogs, news, reviews, etc. Popular usage of this data is in brand monitoring, trend watching, sentiment/competitor analysis, and customer service. However, some individuals and organizations use this data for perverse reasons.

Increasingly, information technology rather than military means will be the preferred method for attacking U.S. interests, attempting to manipulate policy and decision makers by attacking our information infrastructure through selected, discriminate releases via both legitimate news organizations and nontraditional means.

Angela Maria Lunga | Major, US Army, Author of *The Internet and Psychological Operations*

Chapter 4

4-6   SOMETHING YOU CAN DO NOW

As you can see, there are very simple, openly available organized methods to conduct operations inside other countries without those operations ever being sanctioned by a legitimate government. You might think these are sinister and sick, but those conducting these operations are true believers. The chaos and ancillary consequences they cause are not their concern. They intend to win with the strategies you are learning about. We encourage you to seek additional information from the publications cited above to greater educate yourselves. The information is publicly available. Locate, read, watch, and listen to all the source information cited within this *Guide* to make sure you are well educated based on your own research.

> *I think the government has a lot of contempt for the citizens. They have contempt for our intelligence, they have contempt for our need to know things.ml also think that they think they are running us; it's not that they think we're all in this together and the government works for the people and they're a government of the people. I don't think they think that way.*
>
> Joe Rogan | Lex Fridman Podcast #300

Chapter 4

Chapter 4
Homework Break

Please consider all the information presented so far, while seeking additional information and using your critical thinking skills to answer these questions. Write your answers on this page.

1. What sources are cited in this *Guide,* and have you researched them?

2. What information is available from scraping a social media account?

3.   How do you feel about the information you've learned so far?

Chapter 5
More About
Hybrid Warfare

*Real-World Effects of Chinese Information and Influence Information ...
are not just about putting one's views forward in overt or covert ways
in the hope it will change our minds about various issues. Beijing
is much more proactive and systematic than that. Its objective
is to change and shape the way the target (which could be a
government, institution, or individual) begins to think about
or analyze an issue, or what the target's "first principles" might be.
It is also designed to shape the way we talk about an issue,
the presumptive and analytical frameworks we use,
and what kinds of discourse and words are acceptable.
At first glance, all this might seem fanciful,
as if it were some mythical Jedi mind trick.
However, it is much more real than this.*

Dr. John Lee | Senior Fellow, Hudson Institute Author of
Chinese Political Warfare: The PLA's Information and Influence Operations

5-1   BOTS AND CENSORSHIP

There is also something else happening that you can't see and can't explain. It's the combination of cyberwarfare in social media being influenced by bots sharing contrived news stories that focus on reporting selective information. They create emotionality that leads to polarizing an audience. The opposition is censored on social media, and the smaller supportive audience is promoted. Election interference within a nation is a powerful activity within hybrid warfare, and it's supported by the contrived media apparatus that demonizes anyone who brings election fraud to the attention of the public.

5-2   LAWFARE

Lawfare may involve the law of a nation turned against its own officials in the form of what's commonly referred to as "Kangaroo Courts" to silence the opposition. Repressive regimes use the lawfare aspect of hybrid warfare to deny people their rights. This is especially seen in election fraud. The repressive regime changes laws that make fraud easier but claim it is done to make voting fairer. By doing so, the shadowy government develops ways to install selected UniParty candidates who support their agenda with the appearance of a free and fair election. In

5GW, lawfare is the weaponization of laws to destroy the Rule of Law that supports the people of a free nation. Then, it replaces it with favoritism that supports the advancement of globalization.

5-3   POLITICAL WARFARE

Political Warfare is used to change the political position of a country without the use of overt military power. In 5GW the primary tool is PSYOP on a nation's populace to influence the apparent "Will of the People." Doing so in concert with contrived media influence and well managed social media reach gives justification for policy makers to maintain and further their policy goals through domestic laws and foreign policy. They do this based on the manufactured sentiment of the populace.

Chapter 5
Homework Break

Please consider all the information presented so far, while seeking additional information and using your critical thinking skills to answer these questions. Write your answers on this page.

1. What is cyberwarfare? (Go find it)

2. Do countries conduct political warfare against each other? If so, how?

3. Who wrote *Chinese Political Warfare: The PLA's Information and Influence Operations?*

Chapter 5

Chapter 6
More About Unrestricted Warfare

Warfare Beyond Bounds.

Colonel Qiao Liang, Colonel Wang Xiangsui | People's Liberation Army (PLA), China

Authors of *Unrestricted Warfare: China's Master Plan to Destroy America*

6-1   CHINESE COMMUNIST PARTY GLOBAL OFFENSIVE STRATEGY

The Chinese Communist Party's unrestricted warfare strategy is augmented by their Three Warfares Doctrine. Unrestricted warfare and the three warfares are their global strategy, and that strategy consists of psychological, legal, and media warfare. In the psychological aspect, the goal is to disrupt an opponent's decision-making capacity: create doubts, foment anti-leadership sentiments so that the people lose faith in their government, deceive, and diminish the opponent's will to fight.

In the three warfares, legal and media warfare support each other. They develop media campaigns to entice and justify international laws which are subsequently developed into large, repetitive media campaigns to saturate their appearance of legitimacy.

> *The 'three warfares' stratagem is rooted in ancient Chinese strategies of "perception warfare" as well as the Communist Party's origins as an underground and guerrilla organization.*
>
> John Garnaut | Asia-Pacific Editor, *The Sydney Morning Herald*

6-2   ELEMENTS OF UNRESTRICTED WARFARE

The elements of unrestricted warfare are network, law, and economics. Each of these elements have had a preparation phase to be deployed effectively. They will be ongoing so long as they are permitted by fraudulent elections that allow the emplacement of UniParty members who support a globalist agenda that leads to the end of nation-states, the eradication of individual civil rights, and death to the rule of law.

6-3   NETWORK WARFARE

In this fifth generation of war, the degradation and disruption of global, national, and local networks that serve a nation are an easy and exploitable target. The enemy attacks food distribution networks, data networks, energy networks (oil, gas, and electricity), communication networks via cyber based attacks, economic and banking networks, and defense networks, and it disrupts or contaminates the imported ingredients for medicine and household products. These disruptions can happen at minor levels and grand levels. According to the official website for Ernst and Young, a survey of 200 senior-level supply chain executives in late 2020, "The COVID-19 pandemic was a global disruption across trade, finance, health and education systems, businesses and societies like few others in the past 100 years. It is no surprise then that only 2% of companies who responded to the survey said they were fully prepared for the pandemic. Serious disruptions affected 57%, with 72% reporting a negative effect (17% reported a significant negative effect, and 55% mostly negative)."

On September 22, 2022, the Center for Strategic and International Studies reported that "attacks on gas pipelines (Nord Stream 1 and Nord Stream 2) today could foreshadow attacks on undersea data cables tomorrow. In other words, Russia is signaling that it could escalate its hybrid warfare or gray zone efforts against the West—moving from disinformation and influence efforts to a more kinetic direction targeting infrastructure." Network warfare also includes corrupting the human networks of business, government, courts, and education by emplacing extremists or unqualified people to disrupt the efficiency and effectiveness of institutions. Look around, and you'll see it.

6-4   LEGAL WARFARE

We've already discussed Lawfare on national levels regarding election disruption to facilitate fraud. Additional forms of Legal Warfare are employed internationally to conduct political actions through transnational or non-governmental organizations to effect policy that would otherwise not be possible. Once the laws are in place, the intent is to box-in the adversary on the international stage for the purpose of providing deterrents to military action or justify future actions that shape conditions that might usher in a hot war.

6-5   ECONOMIC WARFARE

Anything that weakens a nation's economy is economic warfare. Most recently the global pandemic and the methods used to counter the economic effects have destroyed the global economy leading to unprecedented global inflation and total economic destabilization.

While there is no way to tell [in 2020] exactly what the economic damage from the global COVID-19 coronavirus pandemic will be, there is widespread agreement among economists that it will have severe negative impacts on the global economy. Early estimates predicated that, should the virus become a global pandemic [which it did], most major economies will lose at least 2.9 percent of their gross domestic product (GDP) over 2020. This forecast was already restated [as of August 2022] to a GDP loss of 3.4 percent. To put this number in perspective, global GDP was estimated at around 84.54 trillion U.S. dollars in 2020 – meaning that a 4.5 percent drop in economic growth results in almost 2.96 trillion U.S. dollars of lost economic output.

Statista Research Department | Impact of the Coronavirus Pandemic
on the Global Economy Statistics & Facts (Published August 5, 2022)

Chapter 6
Homework Break

Please consider all the information presented so far, while seeking additional information and using your critical thinking skills to answer these questions. Write your answers on this page.

1. Give three examples of how the CCP is affecting your country with their three warfare's doctrine and unrestricted warfare?

2. What is the purpose of economic warfare?

3.   How much of the media in your country is controlled by state and non-state actors? Provide at least three examples.

Chapter 7
Shadowy Government Destabilization Strategies

There is an urgent need for global stakeholders to cooperate in simultaneously managing the direct consequences of the COVID-19 crisis. To improve the state of the world, the World Economic Forum is starting The Great Reset initiative.

The World Economic Forum Official Website

7-1   HOW TO NEUTRALIZE THE GREY-ZONE FUNNEL

For shadow governments, state actors, and non-state actors to engulf us all into the grey-zone funnel in this fifth generation of war, they must first use the UniParty to remove everything that supports national identity and the right to self-defense. This is a redline that nobody can be allowed to cross; state and non-state actors and UniParty members must respect the basic boundaries of nation-states.

Your nation's economy may or may not recover, but your country and your way of life will not if your country's societal and national identity fall prey to all the PSYOP techniques you've learned here that attempt to force you, your family, and your neighbors into a new normal.

The pandemic was a PSYACT. Who started it? Who are all the entities supporting the changes? There will be more until the people of the world correct their election systems, secure their borders, and feverishly support legitimate leaders, political and otherwise, who support the will of the people.

7-2   THE REDLINE

The planned breakdown of nation-states doesn't have to happen so long as the people of a nation stand up and support the following:

1. Parental rights
2. Border security
3. Election integrity
4. Medical freedom
5. Religious freedom
6. The Bill of Rights
7. Defund UniParty Members and remove them with a fair election process

7-3   ONLY YOU CAN SAVE WHAT YOU LOVE

The redline list and the support of the items is how you save your country and your family's way of life. These items are the redline nobody is allowed to cross. Nobody in the government, no state or non-state actors, and no international body of laws are allowed to cross this redline. Only you can save what you love. Educate others, get involved at the local levels in your communities, organize, and then mobilize. Above all else, exercise your right (and privilege) to vote.

The hybrid threat optimally exploits the environment to prevent U.S. military dominance by contesting the space through unrestricted operational art and portends of replication in the future. The hybrid threat construct offers a framework to describe the evolving character of contemporary war, challenge conformist threat assessment ambiguity and understand the anomalies in the strategic environment. US planning cannot cut the non-linear foot to fit the linear shoe.

Brian P. Flemming | Author of *The Hybrid Threat Concept: Contemporary War, Military Planning and the Advent of Unrestricted Operational Art*

7-4   DO NOT UNDERESTIMATE POLITICAL WARFARE

For several years, Iraq and Iran were at war, eventually nearly decimating the military age males of both countries. Their war ended in a stalemate; neither country overtook the other. After Coalition Forces invaded Iraq and removed the Iraqi President Saddam Hussein and his government, Coalition Forces spent the bulk of their time fighting militias in the streets of Iraq and preventing the militias from fighting each other.

The Iranian-backed militias never believed they would defeat the might, the technology, and the will of the coalition ground troops, but the militias were integral to the political warfare campaign of Iran. Eventually, the Iranian-backed militias seized control of most of the populace through force and fear, much like a cartel would.

While Coalition Forces were busy trying to stop sectarian violence and rebuild the infrastructure in Iraq, it was the militias who were causing continual sectarian violence and destroying the attempts to rebuild the infrastructure. All the while, the Iranian government supported and financed Iraqi political figures. That's how Iran took over Iraq. The country of Iraq still exists, but currently, it's run by government officials who work for Iran. While the perceived main effort of the war occurred in the streets, the political warfare went largely unaddressed, and Iran took over.

What Iran couldn't do for themselves with an army against Saddam, they did in a vacuum with political warfare while everyone was distracted by a ground war. The militias never intended to defeat the militaries of the Coalition Forces. They couldn't. They didn't use conventional warfare; they augmented their political warfare with other aspects of irregular warfare. Their mission was to traumatize, agitate, and demoralize their enemy on the battlefield while the unseen main effort was to take over Iraq through political warfare. Do you see the strategy? Use a distraction, and when nobody is watching, take over politically.

7-5   IGNORE THE DISTRACTIONS – WATCH THE POLITICIANS

In the United States, the strategy is to cause distractions with media propaganda and the propagation of racial and manufactured discriminatory strife to create a scapegoat.

The UniParty has labeled their scapegoat as a racist, bigoted entity. In that manner, they seek to demonize the same group who consequently also denies the fidelity of U.S. elections. Meanwhile, as the distraction occurs, the political warfare goes unnoticed.

This is not a new technique; it's happened around the world in various countries for a long time. For example, the Nazi Party had political reasons for eradicating the Jews beyond a nationalist hatred of their heritage. The Jewish people in Germany at the time were the capitalists and communists in the country. They had money and competing political structures that were not aligned with fascism. Jews were a threat to the Nazi fascist plan.

Hitler used his Brownshirts, formally known as *Sturmabteilung* (SA) in Nazi Germany. They comprised the original paramilitary wing of the Nazi Party. The SA were colloquially called Brownshirts *(Braunhemden)* because of the color of their uniform's shirts, like Benito Mussolini's Blackshirts. Hitler's SA created the distractions in the streets: riots and vandalism combined with anti-Jewish, anti-capitalist, and anti-communist propaganda to develop a scapegoat for the poor post-WWI economy. Meanwhile, he maneuvered his political warfare wing to Nazify the country and seize power. Global supply chain disruptions and broken economies are used to disrupt the status quo and distract from the political warfare that is happening right before our eyes. But this time, the strategy has been recycled on a global scale. It's always the same pattern because it works. It works so long as people don't take notice of it happening and stop it. We are not each other's enemy.

Diagram 7-5
IGNORE THE DISTRACTIONS
FOCUS ON POLITICAL WARFARE
The Citizen's Guide to Fifth Generation Warfare

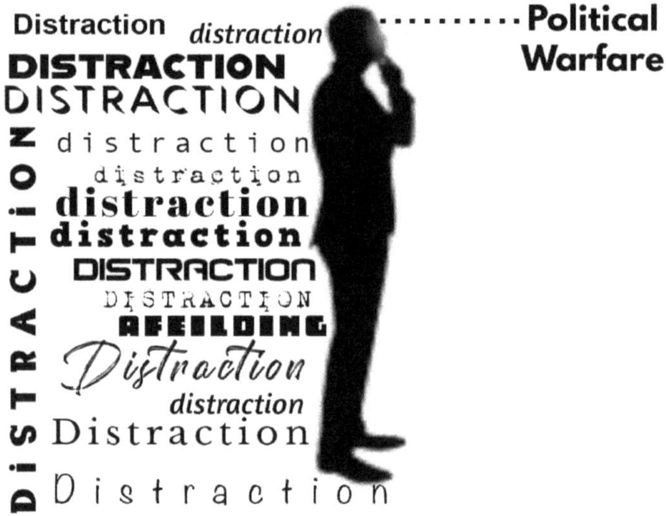

Distraction *distraction*   · · · · · · · · · · **Political**

DISTRACTION   **Warfare**

DISTRACTION

N distraction

O distraction

distraction

distraction

DISTRACTION

DISTRACTION

ΛΓΓΙΙΟΙΝΕ

Distraction

distraction

Distraction

Distraction

7-6   SCAPEGOATS CREATED - ARE THE PEOPLE STANDING IN THE WAY

Watch for the signs of PSYOP. Watch for distractions in the streets by government supported paramilitary organizations and other PSYACTs and the seeking of scapegoats. This is not random or ambiguous. They do not profess the real issues of our time; these are tried-and-true techniques that support the political warfare which is happening in the background. And the scapegoats created are usually the ones standing in the way of their political objectives.

7-7   THE UNIPARTY IS THEIR ACTION-ARM

The UniParty in America is the action arm of the political warfare conducted by state and non-state actors who are working to facilitate a new normal in the United States. Similar UniParty groups embedded in other countries are doing the same. While the citizenry is being distracted by strife, countries are being taken over and rearranged politically for the global new normal. It will be made to appear as if the people are asking for the changes, even though they are not. And while everyone "feels like" something bad is happening, they don't know what to call it. It's called 5GW.

Do not ignore the political warfare that is directly connected to government sanctioned election interference. Learn to identify UniParty factions and the surreptitiously supported paramilitary organizations creating the distractions. Work with your neighbors, friends, and family to make a local action plan. Local action leads to national impact.

Diagram 7-7
THE UNIPARTY IS THEIR ACTION-ARM
The Citizen's Guide to Fifth Generation Warfare

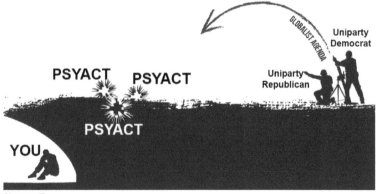

Chapter 7
Homework Break

Please consider all the information presented so far, while seeking additional information and using your critical thinking skills to answer these questions. Write your answers on this page.

1. What significance do paramilitary organizations have in political warfare?

2. What paramilitary organizations in your country are secretly or openly supported by the UniParty faction?

3. What are the lyrics to the song "Bad Moon Rising?"

4. Name three things that can best defund UniParty Members and their supporters.

5. Define: Boycott

Chapter 7

6.   Define: Civil Resistance

7.   How long did the "Velvet Revolution" (Sametová Revoluce) last in
      Czechoslovakia 1989 and what happened during that period?

Chapter 8
Reliability Networks

8-1   SUSTAINABLE LIVING

A reliability network is a sustainable system for living which prevents
basic living necessities from being leveraged against the population to
manipulate conditions of the environment and control the people of a
nation. Having a sustainable reliability network of friends and food
removes the stress and strengthens local communities. Taking this path
is an option at this point; don't wait for an emergency to revisit this
information and get started. Be bold. Don't be shy. Get started
immediately. Find a way or make a way. There will be more disruptions
to supply chains and energy resources.

8-2   CONSUMABLES

Grow a garden. According to the National Association of Gardening, food
gardening, defined as household participation in vegetable, fruit trees,
berries, or herbs gardening, has seen 'a significant uptick' since the

COVID-19 crisis began. The association's research division shares an annual survey to assess gardening activity and purchasing trends in the U.S. The 2022 survey, which is set to be released in the coming days, found that "more than two in five U.S. households (41%) participated in food gardening in 2021 — about 53.7 million households."

If you can't raise your own meat source, find a local source. According to a June 2021 article by Russ Quinn published by Progressive Farmer, Brianna Buseman, University of Nebraska-Lincoln youth meat animal extension educator stated, "People are much more interested in meat production and how these animals are raised and fed, they want to know the local farmer and have a more local experience. We saw increased demand for local meat before the COVID-19 pandemic, and now this trend is even more evident."

Buseman said, "The increased demand for buying meat from small-town meat lockers has provided some opportunities for both these businesses and livestock producers. The resurgence of the local butchers is also good news for the small towns' main streets." And according to Meghan Filbert, Practical Farmers of Iowa livestock program manager, "A silver lining of a worldwide pandemic is it may lead to a more robust regional food system."

Chapter 8

Considering the numerous food production facilities and cattle that have been destroyed in the past twenty-four months, the supply chain failures and increasing inflation, the community gardens and local meat sources make good sense. Doing so removes an ace from the 5GW deck of cards.

8-3   CIRCLE OF TRUST

If tomorrow there was a total breakdown of our banking institutions, what friend do you have who could help you fix your car, pull a bad tooth, or fix a computer? Perhaps you'd have more serious issues and couldn't buy food from your favorite online source. Do you know someone who could take you fishing to get food or let you pick from their garden? Do you know someone who could help an ill or injured family member? You might need people with skills you don't have. Take an inventory of who you know; shore up the relationships with them now. Figure out how to build relationships with people who have skills that you might come to need. Develop a circle of trust by leveraging something you have that they might need. Local people with needed skills in desperate times that you should recruit now are:

- Construction Workers, Electricians, and Plumbers
- Mechanics
- Doctors, Nurses, and Medics

- Hunters and Fishermen
- Military Veterans
- Veterinarians
- Law Enforcement Officers
- IT Specialists
- Lawmakers
- Farmers and Gardeners
- Ranchers
- Ham Radio Specialists

Optimally, locating the people with these skills that are within a ten-minute car ride from your home is ideal, but don't let distance deter you. If it's not possible, do your best. Whatever else you need that's not listed can be found within your circle of trust.

Chapter 8
Homework Break

Please consider all the information presented so far, while seeking additional information and using your critical thinking skills to answer these questions. Write your answers on this page.

1. Where can you get supplies to start a garden?

2. Will you plant in the ground, use pots or planter boxes?

3.   By what dates will you locate additional meat sources?

4.   With whom will you develop your Circle of Trust with and how soon will you shore up your relationships with them?

5. What items, knowledge, skills, and abilities do you have to make yourself needed by the group and make yourself valuable to them?

6. If you are a parent, will you add people to your Circle of Trust who you can pool resources with to Homeschool your children? Other like-minded parents?

Chapter 8

Chapter 9
The Flies Must Conquer the Flypaper

The people are confused now.
They have lived at peace so long that
they do notquite believe in war.
They will learn and then they will
not be confused anymore.

John Steinbeck | Author of *The Moon is Down*

9-1   A TIME FOR MENTAL TOUGHNESS

Mental (Adjective)
a: of or relating to the mind specifically: of or relating to the total emotional and intellectual response of an individual to external reality.
b: of or relating to intellectual as contrasted with emotional activity.
c: of, relating to, or being intellectual as contrasted with overt physical activity made quick mental calculations

Toughness (Noun)
a: the quality of being strong and not easily broken, torn, etc.
b: physical or emotional strength that allows someone to endure strain or hardship.
c: the quality of being severe or uncompromising.

9-2   MANAGE YOUR MIND

The way to utilize MENTAL TOUGHNESS in 5GW is for all of us fearlessly to manage our own psychological susceptibilities that make us vulnerable to unseen manipulation. If you identify a PSYACT, how is it being reported? Is it being reported with loaded language and/or selective information? If the language used to report a situation or circumstance has loaded language, the wording will attempt to leverage the emotionality of the audience through negative connotations, which can be vague. This is a language persuasive technique that often involves the use of stereotypes.

Loaded language has significant emotional implications and involves strongly positive or negative reactions beyond their literal meanings. If you see the use of selective information and loaded language, stop yourself before you become emotionally invested and polarized thinking takes hold of your psyche.

Chapter 9

The same is important when watching videos. Resist becoming emotionally charged until you've seen the entire video, not just a selective clip. Make sure you know what you are looking at by asking questions of someone who knows more than you about the topic shown.

9-3   DECIDE WISELY

Instead of allowing your thinking to become polarized, get more information from trusted people you know who are sensible and from various sources outside mainstream media reports, social media, or internet message boards. If you search online for source information, remember that internet searches are contrived. You'll have to use various search criteria requests and scroll back several pages to find non-contrived search results. Public libraries are great historical information resources because they existed before the internet. Once you've analyzed the situation in its totality, only then can you consciously decide what your position is. Don't be lazy.

Consciously (Adverb)
a: with knowledge or awareness of one's own existence, sensations, thoughts, surroundings, etc.
b: with clear intent; deliberately.
c: in a way that is sustainable, or with awareness of one's effect on the environment, society, etc.

9-4   CRITICAL THINKING - ENCOURAGE YOURSELF AND OTHERS

In a seminal study on critical thinking and education in 1941, Edward Glaser defines critical thinking as follows "The ability to think critically, as conceived in this volume, involves three things: (1) an attitude of being disposed to consider in a thoughtful way the problems and subjects that come within the range of one's experiences, (2) knowledge of the methods of logical inquiry and reasoning, and (3) some skill in applying those methods.

"Critical thinking calls for a persistent effort to examine any belief or supposed form of knowledge in the light of the evidence that supports it and the further conclusions to which it tends. It also generally requires ability to recognize problems, to find workable means for meeting those problems, to gather and marshal pertinent information, to recognize unstated assumptions and values, to comprehend and use language with accuracy, clarity, and discrimination, to interpret data, to appraise evidence and evaluate arguments, to recognize the existence (or non-existence) of logical relationships between propositions, to draw warranted conclusions and generalizations, to put to test the conclusions and generalizations at which one arrives, to reconstruct one's patterns of beliefs on the basis of wider experience, and to render accurate judgments about specific things and qualities in everyday life."

9-5   SHORT CIRCUIT THE POLARIZATION

Critical thinking is a concept with a 2500-year evolution that began in the mid-to-late 20th century, and it's the way we dull the effects of polarized societal thinking that kicks off the path to destruction. Critical thinking short-circuits the PSYOP campaigns that are meant to trick your emotions and polarize your thinking.

Do not freely give away your polarized thinking. If you do, it will be used to achieve someone else's geopolitical goals toward globalization. Avoid a tendency to assume the superiority or rightness of your own social group, also called Sociocentrism, and avoid the unwillingness to consider any perspective other than your own, or Egocentrism.

Critical thinking is, in short, self-directed, self-disciplined, self-monitored, and self-corrective thinking. It presupposes assent to rigorous standards of excellence and mindful command of their use. It entails effective communication and problem-solving abilities and a commitment to overcome our native egocentrism and sociocentrism.

Dr. Richard Paul & Dr. Linda Elder | Authors of *The Miniature Guide to Critical Thinking Concepts and Tools*

Chapter 9

9-6   HACK THE TRICKERY

Meeting in the physical domain is what we call it when we see each other eye-to-eye without the use of an internet-based platform. It means meeting with friends at church, in the mosque, at the synagogue, at the temple, or in other places of worship. It's what you do when you see others at a party, coffee shop, restaurant, gym, tavern, bar, or public house. It's being with others at a concert, political rally, or entertaining event. Meeting in the physical domain is how we break from being imprisoned inside the feedback loops caused by Big Tech that ensnare us and can ultimately manipulate us into mindlessly serving shadowy governments.

9-7   DOMINATE THE PHYSICAL DOMAIN

In the physical domain, you can't be censored and psychologically isolated from others who do not think like you do. And if censorship happens in the physical domain, it's always secondary to a PSYACT that supports a PSYOP campaign in furtherance of a political objective. Meeting in the physical domain is how people hack the effects of digital domain manipulation. Go hang out with your friends and family and purposely do the same with new people you meet.

9-8   NEVER FORGET THIS

Removing books from the physical domain is a known way to control information in order to restrict the ideas of a nation's citizenry, though age appropriateness based on content should be one factor that requires restriction. Eliminating or restricting long-standing food and medicine sources for adults and infants is manipulation of the physical domain; restricting energy sources (oil, electricity, and gas) is a way to manipulate conditions of an environment. All of it will be accompanied by a PSYOP plan that's supported by PSYACTs based on decision dominance in the cognitive battlespace of a nation.

Restricting the rights of people to defend themselves and speak freely in public are no different. Election fraud and mass illegal immigration are shaping operations of the physical domain.

9-9   SHAPING OPERATIONS

According to *U.S. Army Publication ADP 3-0 (2011) "Unified Land Operations,"* "shaping operations create and preserve conditions for the success of the decisive operation." Therefore, restricting the rights of people to defend themselves, restricting free speech in public, eliminating food and medicine sources, restricting availability to energy sources, and promoting election fraud and mass illegal immigration are intended to create and preserve conditions for the success of a decisive operation.

9-10   THE UMBRELLA YOU LIVE UNDER

The PSYOP campaigns you can most likely see happening now that you are through your first reading of this *Guide* all rest under the umbrella of 5GW and are real. We are most certainly all at war. Kinetic operations require direct physical power. A punch to the face or a bullet to the head are considered kinetic. Non-kinetic aspects are means without physical power. Non-kinetic influence happens through PSYOP and the various warfares: cyber, network, legal, diplomatic, economic, political, and media deception.

Now you know what to call it: 5GW. It's worldwide. You are the weapon, and your mind is the battlefield. *The Citizen's Guide to Fifth Generation Warfare* has told you what's happening, how it's happening, and a few of the major players behind it. This is your instruction manual for how to recognize the manipulation. After finishing this *Guide,* you'll be able to spot the manipulation and be able to teach others how to be a cognitive-insurgent so that we can all fight back effectively to disrupt our adversary.

Chapter 9

9-11   TO SUM IT UP

The decisive operation happening in Fifth Generation Warfare (5GW) is movement toward borderless nations with defenseless populations who are controlled by internal UniParty factions who support shadowy governments comprised of state and not-state actors. A nation's UniParty faction will always support the globalist PSYOP plan to create a new world order with PSYACTs, restrictive legislation, and excessive spending.

Identify the Marxist-Leninist UniParty members with your critical thinking skills, and activate your mental toughness to lead the charge and get them voted out of office through legitimate elections. Nothing other than maintaining clean voter rolls, ceasing mail-in ballots and drop-boxes, regulating a limited and effective use of absentee ballots, and eliminating anything other than paper ballots dispensed to legal voters who can provide legal photo identification is acceptable. No more machine voting and no more crossing the redline.

Nothing less can be tolerated to show the UniParty and the contrived media that you are not fooled. Local action leads to national impact, and it's how the flies conquer the flypaper. Finally, boldly protect and consistently teach your children and grandchildren what you've learned in this *Guide*.

Chapter 9

If you don't, your adversaries will teach them a false narrative, and they'll make you the villain.

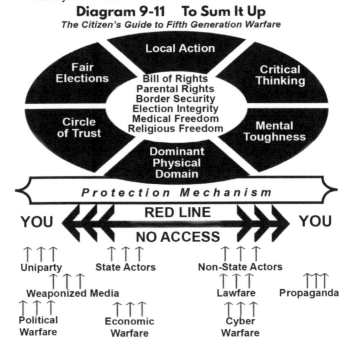

Diagram 9-11   To Sum It Up
The Citizen's Guide to Fifth Generation Warfare

*It is the responsibility of leadership to work intelligently
with what is given, and not waste time fantasizing
about a world of flawless people and perfect choices.*

Marcus Aurelius | Roman Emperor and Stoic Philosopher
Author of *Meditations*

Chapter 9

Chapter 9
Homework Break

Please consider all the information presented so far, while seeking additional information and using your critical thinking skills to answer these questions. Write your answers on this page.

1. Have you noted important parts of the Guide with a highlighter pen yet?

2. Define: Shaping Operation

3.   What happens if you don't dominate the Physical Domain?

4.   What is the most important part of section 9-11?

5.   When will you answer all the Homework Questions? Do it as a group with friends.

5GW Rules for Victory

Regardless of the rules, per centuries of warfare wisdom, we must choose our battles wisely. According to the very famous counselor to princes, Niccolò Machiavelli, the ends always justify the means, no matter how cruel, calculating, or immoral those means might be. He lived in the 16th century, a time of great change and societal and intellectual renaissance, but it was what he wrote about that changed the nature of politics, philosophy, and diplomacy for centuries to come. His ideas about power emanating from a strong sovereign (ruler), someone that could help return the greatness to Italy at the time, was something he knew could not grow out of "politics as usual." If power were to develop, it required a strong sovereign.

In an era of global power politics, with the likes of Klaus Schwab, the World Economic Forum and its associated "Fourth Industrial Revolution," the rise of the New World Order, and the rapid shift by an elite and wealthy society toward globalism, Saul Alinsky's work, "Rules for Radicals," has done more to transform America destructively than any rampaging foreign army could ever hope to accomplish.

What do these two historic personalities have in common? The short answer is

Appendix 1: 5GW Rules for Victory

that they both offer advice on war. Alinsky's reference to Machiavelli in "Rules for Radicals," like Machiavelli's treatise, *The Art of War,* both set readers up for a high degree of ruthlessness and power politics. Machiavelli offers 27 rules of war where his number one rule simply states that "what benefits the enemy harms you; and what benefits you, harms the enemy" (vital counsel for any warrior). While Alinsky offers 13 rules for radicals, a veritable anarchist cookbook filled with recipes on radicalism, Machiavelli issues guidelines for warfare that transcends centuries. Alinsky's monogram offers the principal battle plan of the modern-day leftist counterculture and the politically minded UniParty loyalists.

That said, war is a horrible condition, but like many who have fought in war, we recognize war as a failure of politics. The scars borne out across America and other freedom-loving nations today are nightmarish. Inner cities are destroyed by the ugliness of primarily left-wing power politics, and disastrously failing public schools and broken families (especially in communities of color) attests to a grim picture of American society. And all of it goes unchallenged by their UniParty RINO (Republican in Name Only) comrades on the right.

In addition to the many elements offered in *The Citizen's Guide to Fifth Generation Warfare,* there are ways to counter Alinsky's rules. We assert that our citizenry of democrats are not necessarily all leftists. Equally, a portion of our republican

Appendix 1: 5GW Rules for Victory

citizenry might very well be communist to their core. It is the leftist, globally-minded leaders that are the true adversaries of freedom-loving people. Isn't it time that we go on the offensive, or at least think offensively? We can't keep tweaking and adding more window dressing, which appears to be the role of modern Republicans. Our constitution is under attack, as well as the great nation it birthed, and we stand to lose everything if we don't understand how to counter the onslaught we face from the leftists.

Regardless of our understanding, our words, or our actions, we must stop hiding behind the mask of political psychosis we find consuming us. Ours is a principled and structured opposition, and if we decide to mass ourselves together as a singular America First movement, this must be our governing philosophy. It will take a citizenry of neither Democrats nor Republicans, but those who put America first, who come together to identify, isolate, and remove the globalists and their leftist agenda from our nation. Together we have an American identity that's been forged from the pain, hard work, and intellect of our ancestors that must remain intact for us all to survive.

You'll find a list below of ten rules for defeating these leftist radicals we face. After each, I offer a short description of what each means. Part of our mission is to overcome our own egos. Political activism cannot and should not be a self-serving enterprise. People now must seriously consider their role in this endeavor to save

Appendix 1: 5GW Rules for Victory

America. Stand up, step up, and speak up are not mere words on a bumper sticker. Being an active member of a free society is a way of life for pro-freedom Americans who believe that our country and our constitution still serve as the foundation of everything that is good and right in the world, because they are.

In the seminal work by Christopher G. Adamo,* *Rules for Defeating Radicals: Countering the Alinsky Strategy in Politics and Culture,* Adamo outlines a ten counter-rule strategy that is well worth studying. I highly encourage those who wish to dive deeper into the ideas and underpinnings of 5GW to examine in detail Adamo's well-articulated and unapologetic manuscript. What follows is a listing of Adamo's "Counter-Rules" with a brief description of each. While Alinsky's rules have been used for anti-democratic designs, Adamo's rules are to be applied for good and decent freedom-loving people in America and across the rest of the freedom-loving world. If our society is predicated on "consent of the governed" with a heavy dose of volunteerism, our vision for *The Citizen's Guide to Fifth Generation Warfare* is predicated upon individual citizens becoming much more and regularly involved in the actions and responsibilities of governing and governance. It starts with having an attitude of commitment and the grit to take unwavering action. And it starts now.

Appendix 1: 5GW Rules for Victory

THE RULES FOR DEFEATING RADICALS

Rule No. 1: Never apologize unless an actual wrong has been committed. And then, if an apology is truly warranted, remain very specific as to the issue that is actually being addressed.

When addressing leftists, citizens should never retreat from the truth. Instead, be fiercely unapologetic. The truth is the single greatest weapon we have at our disposal. As this author likes to say, the truth fears no enemies.

Rule No. 2: Never engage leftist leaders and activists for the purpose of persuading them with the truth.

The globalist-minded leftists, especially their leadership, know precisely what the facts are but choose to avoid, distort, or outright lie about them. They are shameless in seeking opportunism. It is also very important that leftists have gotten to where they are, not out of ignorance or due to any lack of truth or facts, which is reflected in their obsessive efforts to suppress facts and truth among anyone who disagrees with them.

Rule No. 3: Never allow leftists to move past their hypocrisy and lies.

Appendix 1: 5GW Rules for Victory

Freedom-loving citizens frequently allow untrue political narratives and hypocrisy to go unchallenged. That cannot stand. In a misbegotten attempt to engage in "meaningful discourse," America First proponents attempt to move on to topics and issues which are wrongly presumed to be meaningful, relevant, and substantive. There is no common ground between the America First citizenry and the leftists. As in war, choosing the terrain to fight upon is something the masters of war always teach. The UniParty loyalists of the left and right are masters of a level of dishonest terrain that is remarkable. Let us choose the terrain and engage in the truth and not relent or be manipulated away from standing our ground. When they try to bob and weave away from a logical discussion, restate the topic and tell them, "You are pivoting away from the topic, and everyone watching you knows it." Repeat this over and over, every time they do it. Don't allow them to change the topic without addressing it.

Rule No. 4: Never accept baseless leftist assertions of "cause and effect," which are vehemently proclaimed as inarguable truth, but are only enabling propaganda.

The list goes on and on when it comes to left-leaning globalists spewing inane levels of propaganda such as, "Children will starve if funding is cut; this move is an assault on women; old people will die as a result of this legislation; millions will lose their healthcare if..., etc." Do not grant them any degree of credibility. Leftists seek to have you accept their presumptions of being on the all-important "moral high ground." When you allow it, you've lost. If you do, any attempt to return to a sane and honest discussion from that point forward is seen as a callous disregard for those they assert as victims of conservative-leaning traditional initiatives. Know the facts, state them unapologetically, and stick to them. Don't let the opposition get a foothold in a logical argument with their nonsense, rhetoric, or hyperbole. They seek victory at all costs and care nothing about the truth. Just because they control the media narrative does not mean they control what is true. Media is a game. Don't play that game; find, state, and stick to the truth.

Rule No. 5: Never reflexively accept leftist definitions of good and evil.

The globalist UniParty leftists believe they have an unassailable right to define boundaries of what is right and wrong; ethical and unethical; civil and uncivil; and frankly, every other standard of morality. They have no anchored standards of conduct or morality. Instead, their standards are wishy-washy and situational, according to what works best for their ultimate victory. Whoever or whatever is most expedient to advance their agenda will be the path they choose. Whatever edict they do choose,

Appendix 1: 5GW Rules for Victory

their flexibility to change it without remorse demonstrates their total and complete lack of standards or morals. When they do try to proclaim moral supremacy, they must be immediately called out. Do not let this stand. Their sanctimony must be bluntly and powerfully dismissed.

By this time, you may be exhausted considering the ugliness and intensity of the leftist onslaught. We argue you should feel just the opposite. We are winning! In fact, their putrid and disgusting arguments about morality and what is right are neither. Instead, once the pitfalls of their tactics and strategy are discerned, clear indicators emerge of just how winnable the battle against the leftists really is. As you sense and take advantage of these pitfalls of our adversary, leave them to wallow in their own ugliness and immorality. Remember, the ferocity with which they voice their opposition reflects fear and hysteria because they know the ideological ground upon which they stand is sinking sand.

Rule No. 6: Power that is not asserted when necessary and appropriate is forfeited. Eventually, it is lost forever.

Moving blindly forward together is exactly how they want us to act. They seek compliance at all costs. An honest assessment reveals how absurd their arguments are and how incredibly slanted the playing field is in their

Appendix 1: 5GW Rules for Victory

favor. This must change immediately. We are far too easily silenced by their vehement Marxist-Leninist assertions that we are not permitted to stand in opposition to them. "How dare you" is their default battle cry; watch for it. If you voice any doubt or criticism in their position, you will be attacked. For instance, the scale and scope of corruption of leftist administrations and the lack of accountability of their side is appalling. Theirs is an absolute abuse of power, and they could not care less what you think or feel, unless you exhibit the courage to speak the truth steadfastly. Stand your ground, and do not back away from the truth. This is what they fear.

Rule No. 7: When leftists rally around one of their own who has been exposed for engaging in reprehensible or corrupt behavior, all who support the individual need to be identified as being equally corrupt, and thereafter diligently tagged as such.

The leftist broad-brush denigration of even the smallest flaws in our nation and its history, thereafter characterizing them as unforgivable failures of America First principles, is a hallmark tactic, and we must stop allowing them to apply it. Do not fall for their traps; some may even be set up as a false flag. For example, every "mass shooting" presents an opportunity to attack the 2nd amendment. The methods of linking every negative occurrence of some event with the right are pervasive among

Appendix 1: 5GW Rules for Victory

the shameless UniParty politicians and their media minions. The leftists' character is marked by being disingenuous, underhanded, deceptive, and dubious. Frankly, it is abysmal, and they lack any accountability for their actions. Our side typically and tacitly allows this abhorrent behavior by dutifully accepting their hypocritical assertions and the supposed need to "move on." Instead, we must stand and speak strongly to their unacceptable behavior and complete lack of accountability in all future engagements. Facing and confronting a bully is the best strategy. Don't "move on" when you should "lock your heels" and force them and their media minions to be accountable. Muster the grit to lock your heels and be immovable.

Rule No. 8: Identify friend or foe. Once a determination is legitimately made that a political player is doing the bidding of the enemy, do not allow it to be altered on the basis of emotion or polished subsequent politicking and pandering.

Sun Tzu recognized in his seminal treatise, *The Art of War,* that an enemy not properly recognized as an enemy enjoys an enormous advantage as long as its cover can be preserved. However, this does not mean that such fraud and deceit only exist on a partisan basis. RINOs have also demonstrated a particular form of treachery and duplicity, but it tends to be wielded against their own kind. This has a tremendously destructive effect on the behavior and attitudes of the conservative movement, and it clearly shows. Described at times as a fifth column, in the political realm, those who don't fight to win don't want to win. Instead, they seek only to stay in power and operate to advance their own egos and bases of power. Any who seek "common ground" with the leftist side of the aisle are leftists and the UniParty as described in this *Guide,* regardless of their stated party affiliation. Diligence, discipline, and discernment are absolutely essential if America First politicians are ever going to regain their footing. Be always on guard. Stick to your principles and values, and be fearless in your words and, more important, your actions.

Rule No. 9: Stay on target. Whenever engaged in an effort to advance the conservative agenda, or seeking to confront leftist fraud and duplicity, it is crucial to stay on point, and not allow leftists to complicate the issue or distract from it.

Much like psychopaths, leftists will never allow themselves to be engaged in a debate where facts and truth prevail. They swim in a sea of narcissistic lies and duplicity. Engaging them in an objective and intellectually honest debate, no matter the topic, is the objective you seek. Do not allow any bobbing and weaving tactics. Laser focus on

Appendix 1: 5GW Rules for Victory

returning to the central and specific issue at hand. Their straying from the center is their method of avoiding the truth. Their arguments will be emotionally charged and invariably totally irrelevant. Simply stated, "Stay on message!"

Rule No. 10: Focus on winnable regions and issues to build momentum and focus on local action that will achieve a national impact.

The ultimate goal is to see to it that the entire country is rescued from existing leftist ideological cesspools and to be set free from the shackles that bind their hold on various communities. The reality is that we must focus on local communities and smartly identify regions of the country where enough of a connection with reality still exists so that the leftist propaganda cannot overwhelm it. We can do this. The goal is not to ignore or abandon conservatives in areas where leftists have concentrated power but work to build energy from the outside in. This is the military ink-spot strategy in reverse. Gain ground where you can on as widespread a basis as possible, and keep gaining momentum.

However, be very cautious of the predictable public opinion polls reflecting overwhelming public support for the leftist point of view. This would be fake news. Do not let it slow down your necessary work. Ignore it, and better yet, laugh at it as you consider their push-back as a verifiable sign that you are winning. The leftists' glaring and actual indifference to any victims of any camp, color, or demographic is palpably obvious to anyone with half a brain. Victory will be to those who are unapologetic and present their arguments from positions of strength and confidence. A no-holds barred attitude is the only acceptable avenue of approach by which to confront them. Presenting the glaringly obvious "cause and effect" relationships of the disasters of the leftist policies and their impacts on people within various locales, regions, and communities are the means to a successful victory.

*Christopher G. Adamo has graciously allowed tremendous liberties and application of his seminal work from his book cited above. The authors highly recommend further research and reading of Christopher's work. It can be easily purchased from your favorite online retail book source.

Appendix 1: 5GW Rules for Victory

Michael T. Flynn, LTG, U.S. Army, (Retired)
BIOGRAPHY WITH COMMENTARY

LT. GENERAL MICHAEL T. FLYNN served over thirty-three years of service in the United States military, which culminated in his position as the Director of the Defense Intelligence Agency (DIA) and the nation's highest serving military intelligence officer.

Flynn dared to oppose former President Obama's false narrative about ISIS as a "JV team" when Islamic extremist groups around the world were growing in number and strength, posing an increasingly dangerous risk, as seen later when radical Islamist terrorist group attacks escalated. Not only did Flynn oppose Obama when testifying to a congressional committee in 2014 (and was subsequently fired), but Flynn also wrote a national-selling book about Obama's negligence, which was published in 2016. And then he had the audacity to campaign for President Donald J. Trump.

Destroying Flynn's impeccable reputation was like a "twofer" for Obama, who was

Appendix 2: Biography with Commentary by Lt. General (Ret.) Michael T. Flynn

also aiming for someone even higher on his list: President Donald J. Trump. Fifteen days prior to President Trump's inauguration, President Obama, then-Vice President Biden, then-FBI Director James Comey, and other senior government officials gathered in the Oval Office on January 5, 2017, to conspire and cover up their treasonous spying on the Trump campaign and presidency while plotting retribution against Flynn. This was an attempt to derail Trump's presidency before it even had a chance to begin. Subsequently, a weaponized Department of Justice (DOJ) attempted to entrap Flynn, but ultimately the case was withdrawn by the DOJ stating there was no crime committed, an egregious demonstration and statement of corruption by the DOJ. However, getting out of the corrupt clutches of the Judge who presided over his case, President Trump issued Flynn a pardon of innocence. At the time of the January 5th meeting in the Oval Office, Flynn was the incoming National Security Advisor and previous Director of the Defense Intelligence Agency and would have thwarted the efforts to undermine the Trump presidency. Flynn was an important key player to the America First movement and President Trump because of his background, knowledge, and determination to expose globalist actions that were not in America's best interests.

Flynn has authored two books: the national bestseller, *The Field of Fight* and *A Letter to America: The Time to Fight for Your Faith And Family Is NOW.* You can learn more about General Flynn at his website: www.generalflynn.com

Appendix 2: Biography with Commentary by Lt. General (Ret.) Michael T. Flynn

WHY I DECIDED TO CO-WRITE THIS GUIDE

First, I was honored and privileged to serve in the United States Army for over 33 years and to have gotten to know and work alongside some of the bravest, smartest, and most courageous patriots on the planet. One of those patriots is my co-author, Sergeant Boone Cutler, an amazing and gifted soldier. If you have never met a true American patriot, go speak to a soldier in the United States Army. They will renew your faith in everything you believe is good and right. I served in conventional and special operations units as well as in several training commands focusing primarily on intelligence, security, operations, and counter-intelligence issues among many other "art of war" disciplines.

I learned an awful lot serving in the Army, but I principally learned more about myself than anything else. As I travel around the country these days, interacting with thousands of grassroots Americans, I find myself explaining to people things I learned during my military training, things about warfare that I take as second nature. From these many interactions, both the questions and my responses, I felt strongly that creating some type of *Citizen's Guide* for the type of war we're facing here at home was not only necessary, but vital.

Those of us who serve in various parts of our government take an oath to support

Appendix 2: Biography with Commentary by Lt. General (Ret.) Michael T. Flynn

and defend our constitution against all enemies, foreign and domestic. In my decades of experiences overseas preparing and training and then fighting to defend our country from foreign adversaries, I never dreamed the greatest battles to be waged would be right here in our homeland against subversive elements of our own government. That said, Boone Cutler and I decided to capture significant and important lessons and skills each of us developed in our time serving our country and share them with freedom-loving people across America and the world over.

I pray this *Guide* allows readers to gain a vastly better appreciation of the different generations of warfare that exist and how the fifth generation of war (5GW) is now impacting our daily lives. Our nation is a constitutional republic where consent of the governed is paramount. We remain a beautiful experiment in democracy, but like our founders envisioned, it can only be maintained by an engaged citizenry. Our families, our neighbors and communities, and our nation and the freedom of humanity globally, deserve our active participation. For without it, we will succumb to tyranny, and like many nations throughout history, we will no longer exist. The authors strongly believe that citizens can engage far better when they are better informed. That is why at this epic moment in history, I felt *The Citizen's Guide to Fifth Generation Warfare* was required.

GF

Appendix 2: Biography with Commentary by Lt. General (Ret.) Michael T. Flynn

Boone Cutler, SGT, U.S. Army, (Retired)
BIOGRAPHY WITH COMMENTARY

BOONE CUTLER served as the Psychological Operations team sergeant in the war with Iraq whose team was responsible for Sadr City (2005-2006). Following the war, he released *CallSign Voodoo,* which was written in real-time from the Warfighter's perspective while deployed to Iraq in Sadr City and during his subsequent two-year hospitalization at Walter Reed Army Medical Center for injuries sustained during combat operations.

Cutler's book, *FPL: Boone Cutler Protocols for Warfighters,* was written about overcoming his prescription drug addictions, fighting with suicide, dealing with PTSD and Traumatic Brain Injury, and pursuing the alternative medical treatments that worked for him and currently work for other Warfighters.

Cutler is the former radio talk show host of "Tipping Point with Boone Cutler: The Warfighter Perspective." He spends his time promoting the veteran and first responder anti-suicide campaign "Spartan Pledge" which is based on the warrior ethos. You can learn more about Boone Cutler at his website: www.boonecutler.com.

Appendix 3: Biography with Commentary by Boone Cutler

WHY I DECIDED TO CO-WRITE THIS GUIDE

I think it's important to get a few things in the open. For one reason, I'm 100% sure the release of this *Guide* will put me on the shitlist of some powerful people who have a lot of powerful friends. The techniques described in *The Citizen's Guide to Fifth Generation Warfare* can easily be turned on me and my family. I expect they will. The decision to co-write this *Guide* came with all my family in mind. I'm sure the rumors surrounding this project will be amazing – I can't wait to watch how it plays out.

Here's the TOP 10 rumors I anticipate:

1. General Flynn and some psychological operations guy are secretly building a militia.
2. Boone is related to the Rothschilds, and he's in the CIA.
3. His other books are satanic, and he's really a Russian woman.
4. Boone Cutler is a white supremacist who was part of a racist motorcycle gang.
5. The photos of Boone Cutler in Sadr City are photoshopped; he never served.
6. Boone Cutler is a plant from the Rockefeller family.
7. His tattoos have secret meanings about Adrenochrome.

Appendix 3: Biography with Commentary by Boone Cutler

8. He's the PSYOP guy working behind the scenes with General Flynn to create QAnon.
9. He worked at George Magazine with JFK Jr., and he is an FBI informant.
10. Boone is a misogynist who hates gays, transexuals, and chinchillas.

Watch it happen. You'll know they are most desperate when they attack my family with emotional-based messaging. We're ready. Halfhearted jokes aside, a few years ago some friends and I (retired Special Operations guys from the Army, Navy and Marine Corps, and former old-school CIA folk) were discussing things happening in America and the world when the smart-ass question came up, "Hey bro, does this shit look familiar?" The resounding response among us all was, "Yup!". Later, when a lot of us were helping get our allies out of Afghanistan after the botched withdrawal, Special Operations folk from other countries joined the group, too, from the U.K., Australia, Canada, etc. We are everywhere.

After the main effort was over in Afghanistan, a chunk of us were like . . . okay, what's next? We were pissed off. We're very smart and superbly trained, and we've seen our fair share of combat. Military veterans love being with each other, and we're loyal to each other because of it. The idea for *The Citizen's Guide to Fifth Generation Warfare* was spawned at that time. Though few know it, we all specialize in non-kinetic (non-violent) warfare, and we're some of the guys who shape

Appendix 3: Biography with Commentary by Boone Cutler

environments (political, social, economic) in foreign countries on behalf of our country. People know what artillery is and what it does, but they don't know anything about 5GW. If we were being attacked with artillery, the proper response would be for an engineer and an artilleryman to train the citizenry how to survive an artillery attack. The challenge here is teaching people what Fifth Generation Warfare (5GW) attacks are and what to do about them. The best people to train the citizenry about the non-kinetic aspects of the irregular war that's happening now come from the Intelligence and Special Operations communities. Ultimately, this *Citizen's Guide* is part of an information campaign that exposes Fifth Generation Warfare.

I contributed to this *Guide* because the method of attack against humanity is my wheelhouse. I'm a boots-on-the-ground guy. Developing PSYOP campaigns and working face-to-face with target audiences has been my game. General Flynn and I are a great mash up because his game is Intel from the highest levels, and the dude has mad smarts. He's also been the target of shadowy government people and groups who used tactics written in this guide against him. He's been a true American, a great partner for this project, and a wealth of first-hand knowledge. If you knew what I know, you'd have an amazing level of respect for the fight he's been through.

It's my duty to protect my family, my country, and humanity from destruction. Whoever attacks me or General Flynn after the release of this guide is looking to

Appendix 3: Biography with Commentary by Boone Cutler

protect and promote the destruction we seek to stop. They can all eat a bag of glass. We will not relent, and attacks against us will only strengthen the resolve of the people who've read the guide and the communities of people who know the information it contains. At this point, attacking us is the same as promoting us. They don't have the resources to win unless they go "full-Stalin" and start whacking people indiscriminately. Even then, it would only accelerate the victory for freedom-loving people everywhere.

The way we win in 5GW starts by educating the citizenry about the war they are a part of in the cognitive terrain that is being conducted by the UniParty, state actors, and non-state actors. Only then can people freely make logical decisions for themselves. That's the goal here. The flies will soon be free from the flypaper.

Now you know my story. Get to work! Thanks for reading. And truthfully, I do hate chinchillas, but the other TOP 10 rumors are bullshit.

All the way! | Boone

Thank you for reading SESSION I

Appendix 3: Biography with Commentary by Boone Cutler

Other Books by
LTG Michael T. Flynn and Boone Cutler

Session 2: How To Fight Artificial Intelligence (AI): THE CITIZEN'S GUIDE TO FIFTH GENERATION WARFARE by Michael T. Flynn and Boone Cutler

How to Fight Artificial Intelligence (AI) unmasks the realm of AI-driven psychological programming and a strategy to combat Ai's invisible manipulative power.

The Field of Fight: How We Can Win the Global War Against Radical Islam and Its Allies by Lieutenant General (Ret.) Michael T. Flynn and Michael Ledeen

The Field of Fight succinctly lays out why we have failed to stop terrorist groups from growing. The core message is that if you understand your enemies, it's a lot easier to defeat them.

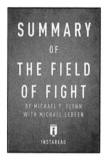

Summary of The Field of Fight by Michael T. Flynn with Michael Ledeen, Kindle Edition.

The Summary of The Field of Fight by Michael T. Flynn with Michael Ledeen includes an analysis.

FPL: Boone Cutler Protocols for Warfighters by Boone Cutler and Geoff Dardia

FPL stands for "Functional Personal Lifestyle" which is a collection of health & wellness protocols put together by Warfighters Boone Cutler and Geoff Dardia for Warfighters (combat veterans) who have made the decision to take their healing into their own hands.

Other Books by General Michael T. Flynn and Boone Cutler

Resources

With our sincerest thanks,
all are highly recommended.

U.S. Army Psychological Operations Process, Tactics, Techniques and Procedures Manual FM 3-05.301

Psychological Operations FM 3-05.30 MCRP 3-40.6

Assessing Revolutionary and Insurgent Strategies, Human Factors Considerations of Undergrounds in Insurgencies, 2nd Edition by Paul J. Tompkins Jr., USASOC Project Lead Nathan Bos, Editor United States Army Special Operations Command and The Johns Hopkins University Applied Physics Laboratory National Security Analysis Department

Irregular Warfare Annex to the National Defense Strategy for the United States in 2020, Department of Defense

National Association of Gardening

Maoism: A Global History by Julia Lovell

Progressive Farmer Magazine

U.S. Army Publication 3-0 (2011) Unified Land Operations

On War by Carl von Clausewitz

A Century of Genocide: Utopias of Race and Nation by Eric D. Weitz

"Politically Incorrect" a song by Tom MacDonald

"Free Your Mind and Your Ass Will Follow" a song by Funkadelic

Quote by Malcolm X

"Red Holocaust" by Steven Rosefielde

"War Pigs" a song by Black Sabbath

Obama's Enemies List and General Michael Flynn in Western Journal by Floyd Brown

"Paranoid" a song by Post Malone
The Road to Serfdom by Friedrich Hayek

Resources

Strategic Monitor 2014: Four Strategic Challenges by Peter Wijninga, Willem Theo Oosterveld, Jan Hendrik Galdiga & Philipp Marten

Quote by U.S. President John F. Kennedy

Anarquismo by Miguel Gimenez Igualada

Conflict in the 21st Century: The Rise of Hybrid Wars by Frank Hoffman

Manual on what to do in case of war distributed to Lithuanian schools by BNS with *The Lithuania Tribune*

Stanford Encyclopedia of Philosophy

Quote by Yuri Bezmenov

Conservapedia Online

Encyclopedia Britannica Online

A Pause in the Perpetual Rotation by Vincent H. O'Neil

Behave: The Biology of Humans at Our Best and Worst by Dr. Robert Sapolsky
Quote by Joseph Goebbels

Resources

Messing with the Enemy: Surviving in a Social Media World of Hackers, Terrorists, Russians, and Fake News by Clint Watts

The Rape of the Mind: The Psychology of Thought Control, Menticide, and Brainwashing by Joost A.M. Meerloo

Quote by General John "Mike" Murray from the article 'Army's New Aim Is 'Decision Dominance' by Sydney J. Freedberg, Jr.

Joe Rogan from the Lex Fridman Podcast #300

Chinese Political Warfare: The PLA's Information and Influence Operations by Dr. John Lee

Team of Teams: New Rules of Engagement for a Complex World by Stanley McChrystal, Chris Fussell (Contributor), TantumCollins (Contributor), David Silverman (Contributor)

Unrestricted Warfare: China's Master Plan to Destroy America by Colonel Qiao Liang, Colonel Wang Xiangsui, People's Liberation Army (PLA), China

The Sydney Morning Herald, Asia-Pacific Editor John Garnaut
Chambers Dictionary of World History by B.P. Lenman; T. Anderson, eds.

Resources

Statista Research Department Impact of the Coronavirus Pandemic on the Global Economy Statistics & Facts, (Published August 5, 2022)

"Three Warfares" official political and information pre-kinetic warfare strategy of the People's Liberation Army (PLA), China

The World Economic Forum Official Website

The Hybrid Threat Concept: Contemporary War, Military Planning and the Advent of Unrestricted Operational Art by Brian P. Flemming

The Moon is Down by John Steinbeck

The Miniature Guide to Critical Thinking Concepts and Tools by Dr. Richard Paul & Dr. Linda Elder

Meditations by Marcus Aurelius

The Internet and Psychological Operations by Major Angela Maria Lunga, US Army

How COVID-19 Impacted Supply Chains and What Comes Next by Sean Harapko of Ernst & Young article dated Feb 2021

Security Implications of Nord Stream Sabotage by Joseph Majkut of the Center for

Resources

Strategic and International Studies dated September 2022

Cambridge Dictionary Online

The Ideology of Twentieth-Century Communism by W. John Morgan, in International Encyclopedia of the Social & Behavioral Sciences (Second Edition)

Continuity and Rupture: Philosophy in the Maoist Terrain by J. Moufawad-Paul

Rules for Defeating Radicals: Countering the Alinsky Strategy in Politics and Culture by Christopher G. Adamo

Here is your special QR code that takes you to a link that is
continually updated with up-to-date perspectives on fifth generation
warfare related to current news topics in our communities like
Big Tech-titans, social media tactics, artificial intelligence
manipulation, and national and international political events.
Provided to you by Flynn and Cutler at no cost.

Printed in the USA
CPSIA information can be obtained
at www.ICGtesting.com
LVHW071139030923
756943LV00023B/399

9 798888 625279